LASTING SUCCESS

What the Bible says about decision-making,
our emotions, and healing wounded relationships

Quality Decisions,
Relationships,
and
Untamed Emotions

David A. Norris

D0878455

Alpha Heartland Press • Ames Iowa

Published by Heartland Foundation, Inc.
1616 Grand Avenue
Ames, Iowa 50010-5353 (USA)

Copyright © 2003 by David A. Norris
Printed in the United States of America

ISBN 0-943177-12-X

THE LIBRARY OF CONGRESS HAS CATALOGED THIS EDITION OF
LASTING SUCCESS AS FOLLOWS: David A. Norris, Pre-publication
Control Number 2002092016.

Primary distributor, McMillen Books
    (www.mcmillenbooks.com)
    1-866-385-2027

The Heartland Foundation, Inc., is a non-profit public service
corporation. For a special education rate or discount rate for bulk
purchases of this book, write to Heartland Foundation, Inc., 1616
Grand Avenue, Ames, Iowa 50010 or lssn@att.net.

(www.emotionsanddecisions.com)—Chapter One of *Lasting
Success* and leadership booklets for maintaining group
dynamic for membership-directed organizations may be
downloaded free. The book, *Lasting Success,* provides the
background for author-led sessions on the subject. Reader
insights are invited and, with permission, may be used in future
publications of this book. Names and e-mail addresses are
never rented, sold or shared.

Hardback $20.95, Paperback $14.95
Canada, add 35%

Readers' response to this book:

As a chaplain I look forward to using this book as a teaching text with its emphasis on the moral component of leadership. Parents will benefit, in particular, from the Bonus Book. It deals with many problems that Americans are confronting today.

—Chaplain Thomas D. Bauder, Lt. Col. CAP

Finally . . . a single-volume collection of life action basics which includes the all-important matter of decision-making and emotions.

—Lois Magee, M.Ed., Career Teacher
Husband, Ph.D., Entomology Sciences

This is a valuable book. David Norris effectively presents the biblical principles that lead to success for the family, career, and church. The goal is a complete and God-blessed life. He supports this goal with decision-making insights that enable us to avoid tendencies that undermine success and cause hurt between people.

—John Stormer, Pastor, Educator,
Author and Legislators' Chaplain

As David Norris' physician for some 35 years, I have been a close observer of his career and family. In this volume he emphasizes the principles that have led to a successful and fruitful life. Our attitude and health are interrelated. I highly recommend this book to success-minded non-fiction readers.

—Lowell D. Bond, M.D.

A very timely book; David Norris presents a universally consistent and dependable worldview. It works because it is based upon the truth of God's Word. Those who study these pages in conjunction with Scripture will find the answers to many of life's most perplexing problems.

—Dr. James D. Fields, Pastor, Founder and
Administrator Cedar View Christian School,
Chairman Evangelical Methodist Missions

Readers' response continued—

Perhaps the first book of its kind, David Norris brings into focus the impact that emotion-driven decisions have on relationships and success. Emotions that lead in the wrong direction are, as he says, the natural product of our old nature. His approach to "guardedness" when making decisions is terrific. It has changed our approach to ministry evaluation and counseling.

—Mark and Denise Nelsen, Missionaries to France

LASTING SUCCESS provides an exceptional outline for prioritizing options available for action, and then deals with the problems of woundedness of mind and spirit. The author understands what forward-thinking observers and students of history have long accepted, that outcomes flow from man's choices in accordance with the laws of Creation and Creation's God.

Mr. Norris' broad experience enables him to share many helpful life experiences in the light of Scripture. Misleading emotions are discussed with an understanding of Satan's influence and God's overpowering provision for discernment and success. To many, this fact alone will be worth the cost of the book. The role of Bible study and prayer in the search for truth and God's blessing are emphasized (John 17:17).

I heartily recommend *LASTING SUCCESS*. It is a valuable tool for personal success and for ministering to the needs of others.

—Ralph W. Hayes, Post Graduate Studies in the Humanities, Doctorate in Education, Professor of Education at Clearwater Christian College, Clearwater, Florida

CONTENTS

—

LASTING SUCCESS

BONUS BOOK

For the Family

for Carlene, our three daughters, and those who follow

FOREWORD

The important role emotional maturity plays in relationships and decisions impressed this writer early in life. Consequently, family, business, church, and government polity have been the subjects of my life's work. Those who know God know that His ways bring a dynamic and an excitement to decision-making. The subtitle for this book could be "True-to-Life Solutions from God's Word."

Additional insights came from an emotion-intensive business career, from several years in crisis management, and in a rebuilding ministry for churches throughout the country. This ministry grew out of earlier requests I had received to speak on leadership.

Determining in advance the short and long-term consequences of choices available involves following God's leading. In Psalm 23:3, David summarized the matter: "He restoreth my soul [mental and emotional health]: he leadeth me in the paths of righteousness [quality decisions] for his name's sake [reputation as the all-powerful God of Creation and redemption]." The focus of this book is upon the reader's future, not the past.

Building a successful future also depends upon knowing oneself. All of us have experienced conflicts and emotional pain. With these in our experience, God's help becomes even more impressive. There are times when we need healing of the inner self. Even the medical profession has come to acknowledge the healing effect of Bible reading and prayer.

"He that keepeth the law [God's instruction for everyday life], happy is he" (Proverbs 29:18).

The acceptance of the reality outlined in God's Word liberates us from making harmful decisions. **A loving and caring attitude toward others reflects the power of God which opens the eyes of the hurting and causes them to desire the truth.**

1. Truth is regenerational: "Of his own will begat he us with the word of truth, that we should be a kind of firstfruits of his creatures [believers should be a testimony to God's grace and power]" (James 1:18).

2. Truth transforms: "Sanctify them [progressively teach believers to make wise decisions] through thy truth: thy word is truth" (John 17:17).

Satan's work to keep the truth from our understanding is apparent in the religious pre-suppositions now prominent in public education, the media, and even in some religions. Secular missionaries dramatize the deceptive "feel good" emotions in order to capture and exploit their victims. "Professing themselves to be wise, they . . . changed the truth of God into a lie, and worshiped and served the creature more than the Creator, who is blessed for ever. Amen" (Romans 1:22, 25).

To fix the brokenness and stop the emotional pain, we turn our eyes back to God's way, the only beginning that brings life. **Those who trust God have every reason to be optimistic.** "Now we have received, not the spirit of the world, but the spirit which is of God; that we might know the things that are freely given to us of God" (I Corinthians 2:12).

ACKNOWLEDGMENTS

For the work of God through Christ, in the life of this writer, I am most grateful.

Several people were very helpful in writing this book. Thanks to God for my wife, Carlene, a true helpmeet for life. She has been a continual source of encouragement and wise counsel. Many years ago when our daughters were young, we built upon the experiences of others and together wrote the chapters on the family (chapters one and two in the Bonus Book). The outcome of our child-rearing endeavor has exceeded our greatest hopes and for that God deserves the credit. Added to the blessing of three precious daughters are nine grandchildren who are home-schooled.

I am grateful to Mari Costella for lending understandability by spending many hours making helpful suggestions and improving the manuscript.

Thanks to Peter Waud, a pastor and counselor, whose postgraduate work was done at the University of Manchester in England. He reviewed the entire manuscript. His ideas for change along with those of Jon Wright, a down-to-earth layman, led to significant improvement. I appreciate L. Duane Brown who was our pastor in the 1970s. An excellent pastor and administrator, Dr. Brown pushed me into a nationwide church-strengthening ministry that contributed much to my understanding. There are others, too many to mention, who have influenced me in ways that made this book possible.

Thanks to Dr. Douglas R. McLachlan of Central Baptist Seminary in Minneapolis, Minnesota, for an unusually penetrating exposition on TRUTH. I am indebted to Dr. George E. LaMore, Jr., Chairman, Division of Humanities, Iowa Wesleyan College. He presented a series of lectures on the ways of God and man titled *A Bicentennial Briefing* at the annual Iowa Realtor Conference, November 1975. I was the vice-chairman of that conference and have benefited significantly from knowing Dr. LaMore. Thanks are also due to the Peacemaker Ministries of Billings, Montana, and the insights of Dennis Reiter. Clark R. Bowers, distinguished visiting fellow at Harvard University, produced an excellent summary of public education, so pertinent to the future of our families. This was a resource for part of chapter five in the Bonus Book.

Scriptures quoted are from the King James Version.

Those wishing to do additional reading about quality decisions, relationships, and untamed emotions will find helpful ideas from the following books: John Nieder and Thomas M. Thompson, Harvest House Publications, *Forgive and Love Again*; S. I. McMillen, M.D. and David E. Stern, M.D., Baker Book House, *None of These Diseases* (guidelines for health from the Bible); and Philip Keller, Zondervan Publishing House, *A Shepherd Looks at the Good Shepherd and His Sheep* (wisdom from the three parables in John 10).

Chapter One

The Best for Life

Abide in me [with spirit, mind, and emotions],
and I in you. As the branch cannot bear fruit of
itself, except it abide in the vine; no more can ye,
except ye abide in me. John 15:4.

The lessons in this book contain lasting principles of great
value to be learned and used in decision-making. Our focus
is God's Word and the role that Christ has in establishing
our thoughts.

The significance of emotional maturity and success came to
this writer when I was a youngster. I was observing a cousin
twice my age who supervised a hay baling crew. He was
engaged to be married and had hired his girlfriend's brother
to work on the crew, but the laziness of her brother
hampered operations. He explained the problem to his
girlfriend and then dismissed her brother. His overcoming
the emotional impulse to keep the brother for fear of
offending his girlfriend impressed me very much.

Happiness does not consist in the absence of emotions but in the mastery of them. As leaders, it is our responsibility to teach those under our care about their emotions. The failure to use our intellect to identify and reject misleading feelings is causing vital relationships to be torn apart. Great pain and sadness result when relationships go wrong.

God gives lasting success to the faithful through the principle of substitution. **By substituting the mind of God in place of our own limited perspective, we learn the truth.** Are we willing to trust God's ways rather than our own? By the substitution of Christ's sacrifice on the cross, repentant sinners are redeemed for eternity.

"Thus saith the LORD unto you, Be not afraid nor dismayed by reason of this great multitude; for the battle is not yours, but God's" (II Chronicles 20:15b).

> What is our goal in decision-making? The goal is to accurately picture the short and long-term consequences of options available for action. We need the truth! To avoid the deception of Satan, the world, and our carnal nature, we must look to the living God and His Word.

God is truth. Emotional and spiritual balance are the foundation upon which truth becomes clear and reliable decisions rest. Christians who know God's Word can feel secure in their emotions no matter what others say or do. "Keep [guard] thy heart [the mind with its emotions] with all diligence; for out of it are the issues [decisions] of life" (Proverbs 4:23). The importance of diligence may be ignored, but the consequences cannot be avoided!

Biblical Christianity and worldly philosophy lead to two distinctly different roadmaps for life. The consequences of sin are sure. Justice is the counter force that places evil in its rightful place. But Christ makes it possible to experience God's forgiveness and healing. "For God so loved the world, that he gave his only begotten Son, that whosoever believeth in him should not perish, but have everlasting life. For God sent not his Son into the world to condemn the world; but that the world through him might be saved" (John 3:16-17).

"For ye were as sheep going astray; but are now [through repentance and faith in God's provision] returned unto the Shepherd and Bishop [overseer] of your souls" (I Peter 2:25). "The thief cometh not, but for to steal, and to kill, and to destroy: I [Christ] am come that they might have life, and that they might have it more abundantly" (John 10:10).

*   *   *

The battle for freedom from harmful decisions and emotional pain has been won; it is but for us to walk in its power. "And what is the exceeding greatness of his power to us-ward who believe, according to the working of his mighty power, Which he wrought in Christ, when he raised him from the dead, and set him at his own right hand in the heavenly places" (Ephesians 1:19-20).

The experience of Dr. Marcus Whitman and his wife Narcissa illustrates the impact of untamed emotions. Dr. and Mrs. Whitman were the first Christians to establish a mission to the Indians in the far Northwest near Walla Walla, Washington. Their mission compound is now a national historic site. Despite their hard work, the Whitmans received many carping letters, and their work was the subject of dissension at annual missions conferences. In time, a measles outbreak plagued the region. Because this disease attacked Indians more often than whites, the Indians assumed Dr. Whitman was at fault. A few emotion-driven Indians murdered the Whitmans on November 24, 1847.

Researchers concerned about productive relationships understand the importance of emotional balance. A good temperament is the characteristic most common among the best corporate leaders. On a scale of 1 to 100, researchers rate the importance of temperament between 85 to 95. The impact that IQ has upon the success of exceptional leaders is much less, rated about 50 on the scale. The relation of technical awareness to success for the top corporate leaders is even less—about 25.

Some common traits of good leadership are as follows:

1. Exceptional leaders are grounded in moral values and proven principles. They study for self-improvement on a regular basis. Personal, social, and motivational skills are priorities. These leaders have a program to educate their people and to monitor progress. This program includes a list of common mistakes and how people will be held accountable. These traits are comparable to the characteristics found in believers who are consistent, who go to the Bible for answers, and who attend Sunday school and church.
2. Exceptional corporate leaders desire to serve others by solving problems without adding needless stress that is counter-productive to themselves and to others.
3. Good leaders are good listeners! They empathize with those above and below them in authority. Good leaders employ people who are qualified to work in phases of the operation in which they themselves are not experts.
4. Good leaders are firm in their leadership roles but are self-critical and seek the opinions of others when formulating strategy. They accept criticism in private without being offended, and are not arrogant.
5. Successful leaders are honest and keep notes where forgetfulness would undermine their credibility.

Research based upon a sample of 5,000 inhabitants of Alameda County, California, brings the importance of emotional peace into focus. Beginning in the 1960s, the researchers monitored and cataloged the people's behavior with relatives, with friends, at church and in other activities. In order to enhance the accuracy of the study, divergent matters such as body weight, smoking and socioeconomic status were discounted. The results were clear: individuals who were least socially integrated were twice as likely to die during the course of the study as were those who had the most stable relationships.

Untamed emotions lead people to believe non-truth. What prompted the writing of this book was the absence of a Bible-based overview such as this and the presence of grief and disfunction that are caused by untamed emotions. It is worth noting, however, that Karl Marx captured the minds of millions by stirring up their emotions of jealousy and hatred and promising a utopia. In the same vein, unprincipled politicians motivate unsuspecting and emotionally immature voters with factional allegations that divide and generate anger. They then seek to conquer the electorate by promising to give them what their emotions tell them they must have. People who do not understand their emotions may be energized by propaganda to sit in a tree for months to prevent the harvest of the tree.

Changes in public education over the last forty years have had an incendiary impact upon the emotions of millions of Americans. These changes include the removal of God from the classroom, the failure to teach established knowledge concerning matters of morality, maligning and distorting of American history, and the teaching of sex education that borders upon pornography in some instances. Most public school teachers are good people, but they have no more control over the above subjects than do parents. We detail the importance of parental choice in the matter of their children's education in chapters four and five in the "Bonus Book."

What is the solution to the havoc caused by untamed emotions? The solution is to ensure that all of our young people, families, and church congregations are taught about the predictable failure of emotion-driven decisions and the rational foundation upon which quality decisions depend.

Chapter Two

Taming Our Emotions

Why art thou cast down, O my soul? And
why art thou disquieted in me? Psalm 42:5a

Emotions are a distinct set of feelings that enter human
awareness and are highly motivational. Noah Webster
described emotion as the "strong impression, or vivid
sensation that immediately produces a reaction." The nature
of the reaction is to either "appropriate and enjoy, or avoid
and repel" the cause for the impression.

> Our will to take action comes from two types of
> mental suggestion: One is common sense or
> rationale, and the other is rationally
> disconnected—the stimulus of emotional sensation.

In other words, emotional feelings can be so impressionable
that a person will foolishly abandon reason and allow the
emotion to control his will. When judgments flowing from
one's emotions pass into insensibility, those judgments are
said to be "more purely emotional."

All of us are confronted with emotional (feeling-driven) temptations that need to be harnessed. Untamed emotions harm both our decision-making ability and our health. "A sound [mentally-balanced] heart is the life of the flesh: but envy [and related emotions] the rottenness of the bones" (Proverbs 14:30).

Detail-oriented people who are unable to see the big picture or are alone and insecure are more vulnerable to emotional entrapment. Emotions are not bound by the principles of logic. A person may experience an abrupt switch from one emotion to the opposite emotion. For instance, when one is not walking in the power of God's grace, the emotional cousins of bitterness and anger can overpower the emotion of love. Likewise, the emotion of shallow romance often blinds the beholder to harmful realities.

> Untamed emotions are conspicuous for causing misleading and very harmful decisions. When we allow an emotion to have priority over rational evaluation based upon predictable outcomes, our minds will then seek to validate the misleading emotion with believable but untrue imaginations.

"Be not hasty in thy spirit to be angry: for anger [and other harmful emotions] resteth in the bosom of fools" (Ecclesiastes 7:9). "For all that is in the world, the lust of the flesh, and the lust of the eyes, and the pride of life, is not of the Father, but is of the world" (I John 2:16).

Scripture tells us that exposure to temptations has a learning benefit. Untamed emotions and imaginations are a consequence of the fall recorded in Genesis. The "do-it-if-you-think-it-feels-good" mentality of contemporary liberalism, secularism, and humanism is the deceptive tool of Satan! This ever-present danger to life, to relationships, and to happiness is very, very real.

"My brethren, count it all joy when ye fall into divers temptations; Knowing this, that the trying of your faith [belief in God's Word] worketh patience. But let patience have her perfect work, that ye may be perfect [knowing good from evil] and entire, wanting nothing" (James 1:2-4).

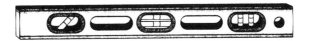

The carpenter uses a level (balance) indicator to keep his project from angling to one extreme or the other. He does this by having the floating bubble in the level in the center.

We must teach others that feelings cannot be trusted and learn from God's Word to distinguish between feelings and imaginations that are good and evil. God then empowers us to reject that which is evil.

Emotions that support healthy and constructive activity occur, but they are not the justification for action. The justification is rational acceptance of the consequences revealed by God's Word. Sin, disease, wild elements, and beasts bring death. The sexual appetite is protected by respect for the lifetime sanctity and value God places on marriage. When one accepts Christ as Lord and Savior, there is an emotional contingent. The justification and peace associated with repenting and accepting Christ is in His payment on the cross for our sin, not in our emotions. Those emotions which accompany righteous thought and action are of course a great blessing. "Whom having not seen, ye love; in whom, though now ye see him not, yet believing, ye rejoice with joy unspeakable and full of glory" (I Peter 1:8).

When we stay humble, Christ gives us emotional maturity, and we find that we can reject the lure of sin-laden emotions.

"Now all these things happened unto them for examples [learning experiences]: and they are written for our admonition, upon whom the ends of the world [evil] are come. Wherefore let him that thinketh he standeth take heed lest he fall" (I Corinthians 10:11-12).

 "But I keep under my body, and bring it into subjection: lest that by any means, when I have preached to others, I myself should be a castaway" (I Corinthians 9:27).

For good decisions we need to retain an inventory of different emotions and the nature of the response they incite. "Do not err [repeatedly], my beloved brethren" (James 1:16). We may have to separate from troublemakers, but, by God's grace, we remain emotionally balanced and reject any rancor toward them. Being spiritual is trusting God for the final result and allowing Him to superintend our appetites according to His Word. Sin-laden emotions and imaginations are the unchecked influences of Satan and the world upon our mind.

> All emotional feelings that arise do so subjectively (they may not have a rational connection). Therefore, we must look upon all emotions with great suspicion.

Responding to an untamed emotion involves a component of faith that is not trustworthy. Faith that is reliable must be based upon a trustworthy object. Those who are grounded in reality and are emotionally mature will identify and police their emotions on the basis of God's Word.

> Simply stated, there are two questions to answer when deciding to reject or accept an emotion: Is the emotion in response to the stimulus whose end product is righteous? Would following the stimulus lead to sin?

Worship has a strong emotional component. However, it is necessary to be discerning about emotions associated with worship. People who are not careful may foolishly focus their feelings for deity in the wrong direction. Even the most talented among us make many mistakes. Gullible Christians who fall into the trap of directing the worship that belongs to God to a talented person end up serving Satan. They will have bypassed a crucial checkpoint—God's Word.

Only God is worthy of worship. The mindset for consistently making wise decisions is a fear and reverential respect for God! "And we know that the Son of God is come, and hath given us an understanding, that we may know him that is true, and we are in him that is true" (I John 5:20a). We honor and respect God's appointed authority persons for the help they provide in obedience to Him. But when a leader type causes people to seek help by praying to a talented individual, or even a Bible character, that leader has violated God's Word. He ends up hurting those who need help by turning their attention away from the only One who is worthy of our prayers and able to penetrate our darkened understanding with the truth which solves problems. "Do not err, my beloved brethren. Every good gift and every perfect gift is from above, and cometh down from the Father of lights, with whom is no variableness, neither shadow of turning" (James 1:16-17).

It is difficult to imagine, but millions of emotionally-driven Russians grieved and wept when the despot Joseph Stalin died. Another improper extreme is total disrespect for God-given authority figures. One could write an entire book about the emotional consequences of these patterns. Protecting our mind involves discernment and a balanced, biblical attitude toward authority.

> We want to protect the throne of our mind for worshiping God and doing things according to His Word! Have absolutely no commitments or alliances that come between you and God.

Not only do we need to identify our emotions, which we must keep in check, but we must also avoid fellowshiping with people whose influence would be harmful.

"Be ye not unequally yoked together with unbelievers: for what fellowship hath righteousness with unrighteousness? and what communion hath light with darkness? . . . what part hath he that believeth with an infidel? . . . Wherefore come out from among them, and be ye separate [avoid exposure to compromise for the sake of holiness in your own life], saith the Lord" (II Corinthians 6:14-15, 17a).

Those who yield to sin-driven emotions in order to experience "something better" end up having less or nothing at all. "But every man is tempted, when he is drawn away of his own lust [untamed emotion], and enticed. Then when lust hath conceived [is not rejected], it bringeth forth sin: and sin, when it is finished, bringeth forth death" (James 1:14-15).

The knowledge and respect for truth makes it possible for a person to have lasting success in spiritual matters. God is truth, and fellowshiping with Him, in praying, and reading His Word are the keys to emotional balance. "For we walk by faith [God], not  by sight [the world's pathway]" (II Corinthians 5:7).

We are made in the image of God. When we value God's Word above emotions (feelings), matters of importance become clear. When we fail to trust God, we invite disaster.

Chapter Three

Factors Affecting Emotions

Delight thyself also in the LORD [and in His precious Word]; and
he shall give thee the desires of thine heart. Psalm 37:4

Problems which God places in our lives are there for our
good. Paul said, "Brethren, I count not myself to have
apprehended: but this one thing I do, forgetting those things
which are behind, and reaching forth unto those things
which are before [God's principles], I press toward the mark
for the prize of the high calling of God in Christ Jesus"
(Philippians 3:13-14). "Forgetting those things which are
behind," "reaching forth," and "pressing toward" are terms
for attitude and behavioral change.

One might ask, "How shall I proceed to be a better testimony
to those around me? Have I trespassed upon the authority
and territory of others?" In this chapter we will review
several foundation stones upon which emotional maturity
and good relationships rest.

TRUTH: God is the only foundation upon which reliable outcomes stand. His revelation unerringly distinguishes between that which is good and that which is evil. Truth is the most fundamental moral category in the universe! God's message to mankind has not changed, and the blessings to individuals and nations that honor the message will not change because it is the power of "the living God, the pillar and ground of the truth" (I Timothy 3:15). ". . . the truth shall make you free [from the bondage of sin]" (John 8:32).

A tyranny inherent in the education doctrine of secular humanism and its liberal cousins is doing away with the truth: impugning the moral value of truth as if it were evil and justifying evil by labeling it moral relativism (Romans 1:18, 25).

"Sanctify them [teach them how to live victoriously] through thy truth: thy word is truth" (John 17:17).

THE IMPORTANCE OF AVOIDING SIN: Sin is separation from God. Bitterness, adultery, murder, and gossip are, in reality, the results of man's rejection of God. Destructive behavior is the consequence of man's proud refusal to let God be God in his life. This rebellion and the consequent corruption are horrible beyond description. Harmony with God is the cement that holds families and other relationships together.

> When love for the Divine Lawgiver is absent from our lives, the emotional bond that empowers harmonious relationships is corrupted. The disobedient sinner views others not as equals but as avenues for getting whatever he wants.

"For the wages of sin is death; but the gift of God is eternal life through Jesus Christ our Lord" (Romans 6:23). The gift is for all, but all will not accept it. "And whosoever was not found written in the book of life [having had no repentance for sin and acceptance of Christ's gift of forgiveness] was cast into the lake of fire" (Revelation 20:15).

The Gospel spells out God's provision for the forgiveness of sin. We will discuss this in greater detail in chapter three of the Bonus Book.

THE CONSCIENCE AND GUILT: The wonderful conscience that God has given to mankind alerts us to the presence of evil. We know from Scripture that sinning and guilt go together. The conscience appears to be an agent of the mind that impacts the spirit of man.

Rejecting the warnings of our conscience is a big mistake that leads to cluttered thinking and more mistakes: "perverseness therein is a breach in the spirit" (Proverbs 15:4b).

Feelings of guilt come when we fail to do what is right or when we do what is wrong. The importance of a healthy conscience for emotional balance and quality decisions cannot be overstated. "And herein do I exercise myself, to have always a conscience void of offense toward God, and toward men" (Acts 24:16).

The condemnatory feelings of guilt cause us to recognize that the sinful act was a moral failure and worthy of punishment. The plea of the conscience is that the wrong be made right. Condemnatory feelings of guilt are a major cause for woundedness in mind and spirit.

Sin and its terrible consequence in the ruin of man are beyond description. Selfish disobedience and rebellion against God's creation are not mere trifles that God can sweep aside. In order for God's forgiveness to be emotionally and ethically effective in our lives, our confession must reflect a change of heart that wants nothing more to do with the sin.

The forgiveness that God offers is not cheap. The purging is emotionally and morally effective because of the efficacy of the substitutionary payment. It is the love, heartache, and shedding of blood by the sinless Christ that paid for our pardon.

> When received, the forgiveness offered by God cancels guilt and lifts the burden of self-condemnation from the sinner's troubled conscience. "Blessed is he whose transgression is forgiven, whose sin is covered. When I kept silence [failed to repent and seek God's forgiveness], my bones waxed old through my roaring all the day long [no peace of mind due to my guilt]" (Psalm 32:1, 3).

Hidden, sin-causing guilt must, of course, be uncovered and confessed before the feeling of guilt will leave. We confront sin with awareness and then, through repentance, place that sin (with its emotional baggage) at the foot of the Cross.

"Pray for us: for we trust we have a good conscience, in all things willing to live honestly" (Hebrews 13:18).

Also, forgiveness cannot be emotionally effective if the counselor or counseling group takes a position of superiority and leads the wounded one to grovel in the pitfall of an unworthy self-image. The truth is, we are all unworthy, but God's love, grace and mercy are all-encompassing, and His forgiveness is complete.

SALVATION BY GRACE, NOT BY WORKS: The belief that good works can save contains two grave errors that create emotional instability. First, belief in justification by good works leads the unsaved away from an understanding of the depth of their sin. Consequently, they do not turn to Christ for forgiveness and the emotional balance that God alone can give. "Not by works of righteousness which we have done, but according to his mercy he saved us, by the washing of regeneration, and renewing of the Holy Ghost; Which he shed on us abundantly through Jesus Christ our Savior" (Titus 3:5-6).

Second, those who have accepted Christ but are still mollified by the justification-by-works concept do not experience the dynamic of God's grace. Some are even emotionally driven to believe that it is their duty to pay for their sin by rejecting success. Sadly, they cannot break the cycle until they recognize and accept God's grace for dynamic living.

Believers are restored to God's blessing for daily living when they confront themselves with self-judgment. "If we confess our sins, he is faithful and just to forgive us our sins, and to cleanse us from all unrighteousness" (I John 1:9).

GENDER PERSPECTIVES: Understanding physical and emotional differences typical to men and women is helpful in understanding relationships. The goal is not to clone the emotional nature of the other person; that would be a mistake. The goal is to attentively communicate with each other and expose from each perspective the issues that come along. When this is done, the merging perspective is often much better than the conclusion of just the man's or the woman's initial opinion.

Masculine	Feminine
Physically stronger	Physically weaker
More realistic	More idealistic
Logical	Intuitive
Objective	Subjective (feelings)
Literal	Tangential
Aggregate thinking	Grasps details
Slow to judgment	Quick to judgment
Do-ers, task-orientated	Be-ers, family-orientated

> There are two worlds in our thought life that impact decisions: One is the world of objective reality, and the other is the subjective world of imaginations. The world of imaginations includes speculating on the intent and motives of others. When unguarded, imaginations inflict havoc.

In the realm of objective reality, the wife has an indispensable role. Men find that their wives often have better judgment in matters of detail. If Moses' father was as insensitive to detail as many men are and had woven the basket that floated baby Moses, the child could have drowned! Wise men respect their wives' talents, and when they listen to their wives, they often gain superior understanding. It is important that husbands speak to their wives in mild tones. Even when spoken in kindness, loud words seem much heavier to women than to men.

In the subjective realm of imagination and speculation, the roles are reversed. Men have the God-given responsibility to be a sponge that diffuses the speculation of their wives. The wife is to listen to her husband respectfully. When imaginative judgments are made, the husband may say, "Honey, I don't believe that for a minute," or, "There is no way that we can know that; let's leave it for God to handle!"

HUMILITY/PRIDE: The characteristics of humility and pride are opposites. People who truly understand the grievous price Christ paid for their redemption are humble. They reject tendencies toward high-mindedness and self-righteousness. The "keeping up with the Joneses" emotion can cause a person to be enslaved by debt.

"Not a novice, lest being lifted up with pride he fall into the condemnation of the devil" (I Timothy 3:6). "Humble yourselves in the sight of the Lord, and he shall lift you up" (James 4:10).

SATAN, THE TERRITORIAL WAR, AND DECEPTION: The battleground for control between God and Satan is the soul (mind, will and emotion) of man. Satan desires to have our mind as his territory (property). People who insist upon self-supremacy are giving precious ground to Satan. "For if a man think himself to be something, when he is nothing, he deceiveth himself" (Galatians 6:3).

Satan proceeds like a parasite and enters the thought life of people (hosts) to manipulate and exploit them for his selfish benefit. "In whom the god of this world [Satan] hath blinded the minds of them which believe not [God], lest the light of the glorious gospel of Christ, who is the image of God, should shine unto them" (II Corinthians 4:4).

Satan's tactic is deception! He influenced Charles Darwin to inflict what may be the most deceptive fraud ever concerning life's origin, meaning and purpose.

Satan exploits the worldly masses with ideas for life practice that cause the people's own ruin. These practices include godless humanism, the practice of deviant sex, and abortion. He was in the thought life of the beautiful and impressive being whom we now know as the serpent who deceived Eve. Satan uses the same tactic today as he did then. He plants doubt about the importance of God's Word and then tempts people by making evil look good, pleasant, and desirable.

"And no marvel; for Satan himself is transformed [through deception] into an angel of light. Therefore it is no great thing if his ministers also be transformed as [if they were] the ministers of righteousness; whose end shall be according to their works [death]" (II Corinthians 11:14-15).

> Satan's power is limited! "But he [God] giveth more grace. Wherefore he saith, God resisteth the proud, but giveth grace [power] unto the humble. Submit yourselves therefore to God. Resist the devil, and he [Satan] will flee from you" (James 4:6-7).

LIBERTY: Real liberty is freedom from the deceptive control of our old nature, Satan, and the world. The context of liberty is a life-enhancing environment. The Bible is the source for life-enhancing principles and emotions for wise decisions.

> "Love not the world, neither the things that are in the world. If any man love the world, the love of the Father is not in him. For all that is in the world, the lust of the flesh, and the lust of the eyes, and the pride of life, is not of the Father, but is of the world" (I John 2:15-16). "This I say then, Walk in the Spirit, and ye shall not fulfill the lust [emotions] of the flesh" (Galatians 5:16).

SEPARATION: The distinction between the ways of God and man is covered in the doctrine of separation. Be not deceived—spiritual and emotional health for lasting success requires God-honoring separation from the ways of the world.

Some clergy fellowship and participate in teaching ministries with evangelicals who teach contrary to God's Word. Those who buy that idea open their minds, as well as their children's, to compromise with the world. They pay a high spiritual price that can run through their family for many generations!

The apostle Paul declared, "For I know this, that after my departing shall grievous wolves enter in among you, not sparing the flock. Also of your own selves shall men arise, speaking perverse things, to draw away disciples after them. Therefore watch, and remember, that by the space of three years I ceased not to warn every one night and day with tears" (Acts 20:29-31). "Prove all things; hold fast that which is good. Abstain from all appearance of evil" (I Thessalonians 5:21-22). The difference between living according to God's Word and compromising His Word is not a fine line—it is a chasm!

STRONGHOLDS: Satan's strongholds are the worldly values that people hold in their minds. Prior to his violent death, a young man once told me, "Satan is playing me like a yo-yo." This young man had been accepting worldly values into his mind, and Satan was using them to destroy him.

God cannot honor and empower us when we meddle with sin. Sin in our lives enables Satan to attach himself and influence our thinking. Pulling down strongholds is the work of God through Christ. By His indwelling Spirit, God empowers believers to recognize and cast out evil imaginations (replacing evil thoughts with good).

We must trust God's Word, not our emotions or feelings. "For though we walk in the flesh [we are human], we do not war after [by the power of] the flesh: (For the weapons of our warfare are not carnal, but mighty through God to the pulling down of strong holds;) Casting down imaginations, and every high thing that exalteth itself against the knowledge of God, and [wisely] bringing into captivity every thought [replacing evil thoughts with righteous thoughts] to the obedience of Christ" (II Corinthians 10:3-5).

Satan becomes powerless when we bring our problems to God in the name of Christ. "But if we walk in the light, as he is in the light, we have fellowship one with another, and the blood of Jesus Christ his Son cleanseth us from all sin" (I John 1:7). "Ye are of God, little children, and have overcome them: because greater is he [Christ's Spirit] that is in you, than he [Satan] that is in the world" (I John 4:4).

> Untamed emotions are Satan's stronghold. Sin-laden emotions entrap and mislead a person because they cause the human mind to support the distortions with believable but faulty imaginations!

PRINCIPALITIES: This refers to leaders who conspire to deceive and exploit mankind.

"For we wrestle not against flesh and blood, but against principalities, against powers, against the rulers of the darkness of this world, against spiritual wickedness in high places. Wherefore take unto you the whole armor of God [clothe yourself], that ye may be able to withstand in the evil day, and having done all, to stand [yielding no ground to Satan]. Stand therefore, having your loins girt about with truth [God's Word], and having on the breastplate of righteousness; And your feet shod with the preparation of the gospel of peace; Above all, taking the shield of faith [God's Word never fails], wherewith ye shall be able to quench all the fiery darts [strategies and deception] of the wicked. And take the helmet of salvation , and the sword of the Spirit, which is the word of God: Praying always [continually] with all prayer and supplication [for direction] in the Spirit, and watching thereunto with all perseverance [so you will always be walking according to God's Word] and supplication for all saints" (Ephesians 6:12-18).

> **"The secret of the LORD is with them that fear him; and he will show them his covenant" (Psalm 25:14). "Trust in the LORD with all thine heart; and lean not unto thine own understanding. In all thy ways acknowledge him, and he shall direct thy paths" (Proverbs 3:5-6).**

GRACE, EMOTIONAL MATURITY, AND DECISION-MAKING: Grace brings us to the true nature of God.

First, on the basis of Christ's sacrifice spoken of in John 3:16, God has provided the way to forgive our sin and give us eternal life. Offered by God, this is an awesome gift and the greatest of all possible personal blessings. Christ's sinless nature was imputed to our account. Not having to pay for our sin is the merciful aspect of God's grace.

"Whom God hath set forth to be a propitiation [sacrifice] through faith in his blood, to declare his righteousness for the remission of sins that are past, through the forbearance of God" (Romans 3:25).

Second, every born-again believer is entitled to pray directly to God through Jesus Christ, our High Priest. We are freed from bondage to any human intermediary. "And from Jesus Christ, who is the faithful witness, and the first begotten of the dead, and the prince of the kings of the earth. Unto him that loved us, and washed us from our sins in his own blood, And hath made us kings and priests unto God and his Father; to him be glory and dominion for ever and ever. Amen" (Revelation 1:5).

"Let us therefore come boldly unto the throne of grace, that we may obtain mercy [for when we fail and sin], and find grace to help [overcome temptation] in time of need" (Hebrews 4:16).

Third, because of God's grace, our eyes and heart are enlightened. Grace makes wise decisions and emotional balance possible. We can see in advance and resist the wiles of Satan, the old nature, and the world.

"The eyes of your understanding being enlightened; that ye may know what is the hope of his calling, and what the riches of the glory of his inheritance in the saints, And what is the exceeding greatness of his power to us-ward who believe, according to the working of his mighty power, Which he wrought in Christ, when he raised him from the dead, and set him at his own right hand in the heavenly places, Far above all principality, and power, and might, and dominion, and every name that is named, not only in this world, but also in that which is to come" (Ephesians 1:18-21).

Fourth, believers are empowered by God's grace to share the supernatural power of His love, to forgive (not be emotionally disturbed by) offenders and to keep a clear mind. The only way a Christian can fail to be so empowered is by displacing God's grace with the rebellion and emotional stubbornness of self-will.

"That Christ may dwell in your hearts by faith; that ye, being rooted and grounded in love, May be able to comprehend with all saints what is the breadth, and length, and depth, and height; And to know the love of Christ, which passeth knowledge, that ye might be filled with all the fulness of God. Now unto him that is [present tense] able to do exceeding abundantly above all that we ask or think, according to the power that worketh in us" (Ephesians 3:17-20).

Fifth, because of God's grace, faithful believers benefit spiritually and grow stronger through setbacks and disappointing experiences. We must keep up our faith in God. The crises that we have experienced or are now going through are not the greatest danger to us. Unbelief is a greater setback than any other problem we can ever experience.

"Ye are of God, little children, and have overcome them: because greater is he [Christ] that is in you, than he [Satan] that is in the world" (I John 4:4).

Sixth, we can rest in peace because victory over our enemies, including the sin nature within, is assured. "Seeing it is a righteous thing with God to recompense tribulation to them that trouble you; And to you who are troubled rest [in His promises] with us, when the Lord Jesus shall be revealed from heaven with his mighty angels" (II Thessalonians 1:6-7).

"Who shall lay any thing to the charge of God's elect [born-again believers]? It is God that justifieth. Who is he that condemneth? It is Christ that died [in payment for sin], yea rather, that is risen again, who is even at the right hand of God, who also maketh intercession for us. Who shall separate us from the love [grace] of Christ? shall tribulation, or distress, or persecution, or famine, or nakedness, or peril, or sword? As it is written, For thy sake we are killed all the day long [judgment for our sin, the barrier to victory, is continually displaced by the substitutionary death of Christ]; we [our old natures] are accounted as sheep for the slaughter. Nay, in all these things we are more than conquerors through him [Christ, the spotless Lamb] that loved us. For I am persuaded, that neither death, nor life, nor angels, nor principalities, nor powers, nor things present, nor things to come, Nor height, nor depth, nor any other creature, shall be able to separate us from the love of God, which is in Christ Jesus our Lord" (Romans 8:33-39).

Seventh, the Christ-like love and power He gives us to forgive others assures us that our relationship with God is real. If this is not true in your life, we have summarized God's provision for salvation, the new spiritual birth in Christ, in chapter three of the Bonus Book.

"No man hath seen God at any time. If we love one another, God dwelleth in us, and his love is perfected in us. Hereby know we that we dwell in him, and he in us, because he hath given us of his Spirit" (I John 4:12-13).

GRACE "I AMs" FOR THE SAVED (modified from Bible Word computer outline):

- I am a child of God (John 1:12).
- I am a citizen of heaven (Philippians 3:20).
- I am more than a conqueror (Romans 8:37).
- I am a joint heir with Christ, with an inheritance from God (Ephesians 1:18).
- I am reconciled to God (II Corinthians 5:18-19).
- I am a member of God's royal priesthood (I Peter 2:9).
- I am the dwelling-place of God's Spirit (I Corinthians 3:16).
- I am free forever from condemnation (Romans 8:1).
- I am justified; God has declared me righteous (Romans 8:30).
- I am complete in Christ (Colossians 2:10).

> "And this is the record, that God hath given to us eternal life, and this life is in his Son. He that hath the Son hath life; and he that hath not the Son of God hath not life. **These things have I written unto you that believe on the name of the Son of God; that ye may KNOW that ye have eternal life**, and that ye may believe [without reservation] on the name of the Son of God" (I John 5:11-13).

FEAR: It is important that Christians learn to confront, evaluate and manage the emotion of fear. Fear of God is good. The Bible tells us that "The fear of the LORD is the beginning of wisdom" (Psalm 111:10a). "The fear of the LORD is clean, enduring for ever: the judgments of the LORD are true and righteous altogether" (Psalm 19:9). Godless humanist concepts for counteracting fear can be propped up for a time, but eventually the props collapse, and the frightful hammer of truth falls upon the wicked.

"And deliver them who through fear of death were all their lifetime subject to bondage [brought down]" (Hebrews 2:15). Christ said, "And fear not them which kill the body, but are not able to kill the soul: but rather fear him which is able to destroy both soul and body in hell" (Matthew 10:28). "Yea, though I walk through the valley of the shadow of death, I will fear no evil: for thou art with me; thy rod and thy staff they comfort me" (Psalm 23:4). "But now thus saith the LORD that created thee . . . Fear not: for I have redeemed thee, I have called thee by thy name; thou art mine" (Isaiah 43:1).

• The fear of failure is greatly reduced if we become a God-honoring leader at home. Home is where we develop the empathy, power, love, and understanding needed to succeed outside the home.

"Let the deacons be the husbands of one wife, ruling their children and their own houses well" (I Timothy 3:12). Husbands and wives submit to one another, but the husband is the final arbitrator of what is to be done. As leaders, on that point, we must not be mean but kindly firm. We learn to lead large groups by first ruling our ". . . own house, [lovingly] having his [our] children in subjection [without provoking them to wrath] with all gravity" (I Timothy 3:4). "In God [whose Word never fails] have I put my trust: I will not be afraid [of] what man can do unto me. Thy vows are upon me, O God: I will render praises unto thee" (Psalm 56:11-12).

• Beyond the help of parents and one's spouse, trusted people in the work place who will edify can also reduce our reasons for fear. Like the wife who becomes the eyes and ears regarding the children's safety, trusted associates at work are your support team. There is no need to be embarrassed about unintended mistakes. The story is told about a dinner gathering held by the soon-to-be-president of the United States, Dwight Eisenhower. At the start of a testimonial time, men were praising him, but he slowed them down by saying something like this: "I have feet of clay just like everyone else. I am depending upon you to come to me in private and share your concern with me when you see me moving in what appears to be the wrong direction. Sometimes your input will change my assessment; sometimes it will not. If you value what we are here to accomplish, you will be honest with me. "For God hath not given us the spirit of fear; but of power, and of love, and of a sound [sensible, stable] mind" (II Timothy 1:7).

• The fear of people is diminished when we realize that others have insecurities just as we do. Let love and concern for others overcome self-consciousness. "There is no fear in love; but perfect love casteth out fear: because fear hath torment. He that feareth is not made perfect in love" (I John 4:18).

• Failure to keep debt at a safe level creates fear. Keep finances in order, get your rest, and enjoy your family. When problems get the upper hand, you still have a haven of rest.

• Avoid rebellion against your God-given authorities. Our first obligation is directly to God. You may disagree with a God-given authority person in matters of objective reality, but hold them in your heart with respect for the role God has given them. "What time I am afraid, I will trust in thee" (Psalm 56:3).

• The subject of much of God's Word concerns keeping one's life pure. People become decision-impaired and fearful when living in sin. A person I knew had been involved in an adulterous relationship. Influenced by prayers and God's Spirit, he received Christ. He repented of his sin to God and to his wife, who forgave him. Later he wisely called the other woman, apologized, and asked her forgiveness. If we sin against a person by stealing, gossiping, etcetera, we must go to that person and confess the sin to the person and to God (I John 1:9). Jesus paid for our sin.

ANGER AND ITS COUSINS:
There is a proper time and reason for showing anger. When a person is controlled by the Holy Spirit the anger will be displayed in love and God-directed.

"Be ye angry [righteous anger], and sin not: let not the sun go down upon your wrath" (Ephesians 4:26).

The human emotion of anger, however, is man's enemy. "He that is of a proud heart stirreth up strife: but he that putteth his trust in the LORD shall be made fat [content and prosperous]" (Proverbs 28:25). When considering the devastation anger imposes upon one's judgment, we may think of the murders attributed by some to O. J. Simpson. Two persons suffered tragic deaths, and millions of dollars were lost in reputation and earning power.

Anger's first cousin is perhaps jealousy or envy, followed by bitterness, harsh language, wrath, and ultimately the will to murder. Tolerance for anger is a self-destroying sin. "Be not hasty in thy spirit to be angry: for anger resteth [causes turmoil] in the bosom of fools" (Ecclesiastes 7:9).

What more can be said about anger? "We know that we have passed from death unto life [spiritual life], because we love the brethren. He that loveth not his brother abideth in death [is spiritually dead]" (I John 3:14).

Deal with anger and other sins in the following ways:

1. Distrust your selfish nature. It will betray you every time. Kick the old nature off the throne of your life.
2. Get out of God's way. Make a list of sin-laden emotions. Ask God to forgive you for trusting in self rather than in Him for truth and lasting success. The human mind is no match for the deception of Satan and the world.
3. Worship God in your heart. Dwell on His Word when confronted by offensive situations. "Be careful [anxious] for nothing; but in every thing by prayer and supplication with thanksgiving let your requests be made known unto God. And the peace of God, which passeth all understanding, shall keep your hearts and minds through Christ Jesus" (Philippians 4:6-7).

"Finally, brethren, whatsoever things are true, whatsoever things are honest, whatsoever things are just, whatsoever things are pure, whatsoever things are lovely, whatsoever things are of good report; if there be any virtue, and if there be any praise, think on these things" (Philippians 4:8).

4. Without prescribing what, when, or how, place your total trust in the sovereignty, power, and will of God for decisions! Be thankful and rest in Christ. "For to be carnally minded is death; but to be spiritually minded [walking by faith in Christ's ways] is life and peace" (Romans 8:6).

JUDGMENTALISM AND ITS COUSINS: An August 25, 1999, headline in *USA Today* read, "Holding a Grudge Is Hazardous to Your Health." The article by Mairlyn Elias went on to say, "Growing evidence shows that people inclined to forgive others enjoy better mental and physical health than those who hold grudges. Angry people have the most trouble forgiving." Those who are honest about their own shortcomings "forgive readily." Those who ask forgiveness of others for misdeeds do not make the mistake of blaming others for their own misdeeds. This is news to many, but for over 2000 years people who read the Bible have known this. People who pass over and ignore a transgression imposed by another are not weak. They are strong and wise.

"By long forbearing [quiet patience] is a prince persuaded, and a soft tongue breaketh the bone [leaves the transgressor feeling his guilt]" (Proverbs 25:15). "Make no friendship with an angry man; and with a furious man thou shalt not go; Lest thou learn his ways, and get a snare to thy soul" (Proverbs 22:24-25).

We now go to the important role of a balanced self-image: "Am I at peace with myself?"

Chapter Four

Deliver Me From All My Fears

I sought the LORD, and he heard me, and
delivered me from all my fears. Psalm 34:4

The attitude we have toward ourselves has a big influence,
helpful or harmful, upon the attitudes we have toward
God, family, and friends. A negative and conflicted view
of self impairs our ability to proceed and be successful.

I was raised in a Friends (Quaker) Church environment. Our
pastor brought in a Baptist evangelist, and it was then at the
age of seven that I invited Christ into my life. I am grateful
for the ministry of that little church, for it was there that I
was taught to understand and fear sin. However, the church
was peculiarly pietistic, which impacted my self-image. The
meaning of humility was exaggerated, and poverty seemed
to be looked upon as a virtue. It was several years before I
figured out that it was acceptable to have material success,
and I still find it difficult to accept praise.

Many years later as an employer, I noticed that our secretary, who was going through a phase of excess in dress and make-up, was downhearted. One day when she brought some papers into my office, I casually mentioned that she seemed rather blue and asked if I could be of some encouragement.

Peg (a fictitious name) sat down and told me the situation. In short, what had happened was that she had experienced an honorable courtship with a young man, and they had planned to be married. However, he took a trip abroad, met another girl and jilted Peg.

Hearing her story, it became clear why she was so gloomy. It also explained why she had changed and was over dressing and using too much make-up. Unlike my self-image distortion, which had been acquired over time, Peg's self-rejection resulted from a single incident—the loss of her fiancé. Peg was so wounded and confused by the loss that her judgment became distorted. Her inability to think clearly led, in turn, to a spiritual dysfunction. She was, by the definition used in this book, wounded in spirit.

Peg was a pretty girl, but there are some who are not. Self-rejection can come from feelings that one's appearance or family background is inferior, from sin, or from serious personal failure.

In Peg's woundedness, she came to the mistaken conclusion that she was not pretty enough to retain a boyfriend's loyalty. The controlling thought that followed was that if God had made a mistake in creating her appearance, how could she depend upon God? She couldn't be successful.

We then talked about her new future. There were two young men who had shown interest in her and a third who had moved away but had left a good impression. A letter by Peg suggesting correspondence was sent to the latter young man, and we agreed to give him a month to respond.

When no reply came he was marked off the list. Soon Peg was asked for a date to go biking with another young man. We agreed that she would dress very casual and trust God for a mate who would take her as she was.

Peg found Romans 8:28 to be true. Within a couple of years, she became the wife of a good young man. Following the wedding, Peg's father, whom I had not previously met, came and thanked me for my part during the difficult time in her life. Peg and her husband are now a happy Christian family with two teenagers.

> Judging our worth or acceptability by comparing ourselves with others is a mistake. God has made each of us with unique and exceptional gifts. Where some excel, we may not; where we excel, others may not.

"For we dare not . . . compare ourselves with some that commend themselves: but they . . . comparing themselves among themselves, are not wise [do not understand God's way]" (II Corinthians 10:12).

Having a God-honoring attitude makes a disadvantaged background or seemingly impossible problems become small. The Lord planned our parents, our siblings and our situation in life. "For we are his workmanship, created in Christ Jesus unto good works, which God hath before ordained that we should walk in them" (Ephesians 2:10).

The story is told about Ethel Waters, the soloist, who had been asked how it was that she had become so successful in a racially prejudiced environment. Referring to her skin color, she then credited and quoted her father, "God don't make no mistakes." Consider also the homely, back-country Abraham Lincoln and the short, heavy-set John Adams who, despite their disadvantages, became presidents of the United States.

"I will praise thee; for I am fearfully and wonderfully made: marvelous are thy works; and that my soul knoweth right well. My substance was not hid from thee when I was made in secret, and curiously wrought in the lowest parts of the earth. Thine eyes did see my substance, yet being unperfect; and in thy book all my members were written, which in continuance were fashioned, when as yet there was none of them. How precious also are thy thoughts unto me, O God! How great is the sum of them!" (Psalm 139:14-17).

"So that we may boldly say [and believe in our heart], The Lord [our Creator] is my helper [strength], and I will not fear what man shall do unto me" (Hebrews 13:6).

Setbacks and disadvantages give us the opportunity to learn about God's overcoming power. Our problems give God the opportunity to develop in us the character and endurance needed for success. "And lest I should be exalted above measure through the abundance of the revelations [pride], there was given to me a thorn [unfavorable condition] in the flesh, the messenger of Satan [would test my faith] to buffet me, lest I should be exalted above measure" (II Corinthians 12:7).

Happiness is the product that results when our focus is upon the needs of others, when we encourage them and help them to know the mind of God. "Ye are our epistle written in our hearts, known and read of all men" (II Corinthians 3:2.) "Therefore, my brethren dearly beloved and longed for, my joy and crown, so stand fast in the Lord, my dearly beloved" (Philippians 4:1).

"For it is God which worketh in you both to will and to do of his good pleasure" (Philippians 2:13). "Rejoice evermore [God is in control]. Pray without ceasing fellowship with the living God]. In every thing give thanks: for this is the will of God in Christ Jesus concerning you" (I Thessalonians 5:16-18).

Chapter Five

Emotions, Relationships, & Prayer

The prayer of the upright is his delight.
Proverbs 15:8b

God brings difficulties into our lives to build character and to strengthen our faith. Learning the value of prayer is part of the character building process. The fact that humans are enormously complex is no barrier to God. He formed the laws upon which relationships hinge. **Prayer and love are the foundation blocks upon which emotional balance and relationships stand**.

The importance of prayer is more readily appreciated when we realize that God is in the business of making choices. He makes choices that reflect His power for good in the lives of the faithful. "For I know the thoughts [plans] that I think toward you, saith the LORD, thoughts of peace [perform My good toward you], and not of evil, to give you an expected end [hope and a future]" (Jeremiah 29:11).

God is at work in every age accomplishing His purposes and fulfilling His plan. Although mistakes may have interim consequences, God, Who is gracious and all powerful, sees to it ". . . that all things [which happen to believers, good or bad, ultimately] work together for good to them that love God, to them who are the called according to his purpose" (Romans 8:28).

The lives of forward-moving Christians illustrate the steadiness of mind that comes with trust in God's plan and direction. In the midst of trouble, those who are faithful are learners and overcomers. "And Joseph [after many tears] said unto his brethren, Come near to me, I pray you. And they came near. And he said, I am Joseph your brother, whom ye sold [as a slave] into Egypt" (Genesis 45:4). Later, "And when Joseph's brethren saw that their father was dead, they And said, Joseph will peradventure hate us, and will certainly requite [avenge] us all the evil which we did unto him . . . And Joseph said unto them, Fear not: for am I [I am not] in the place of God? But as for you, ye thought evil against me; but God meant it [purposed it] unto good, to bring to pass, as it is this day, to save much people alive" (Genesis 50:15, 19-20).

Our appreciation for the value of prayer grows when we realize that God is an emotional being and that He cares. He experienced the same emotions that we experience, such as:

Joy—"as the bridegroom rejoiceth over the bride, so shall thy God rejoice over thee" (Isaiah 62:5b).

Sorrow—"and his soul was grieved for the misery of Israel" (Judges 10:16b).

Compassion—"The LORD is gracious, and full of compassion; slow to anger, and of great mercy. The LORD is good to all: and his tender mercies are over all his works" (Psalm 145:8-9).

Anger—"And when he [Christ] had looked round about on them with anger, being grieved for the hardness of their hearts, he saith unto the man, Stretch forth thine hand" (Mark 3:5a).

"Seeing then that we have a great high priest, that is passed into the heavens, Jesus the Son of God, let us hold fast our profession [fellowship with God]. **For we have not an high priest which cannot be touched with the feeling of our infirmities; but was in all points tempted like as we are, yet without sin" (Hebrews 4:14-15)**.

God loves us even more than we love ourselves and is sensitive to our prayers. When I was in sixth grade our school merged with another in the town of Indianola, Iowa. I became acquainted with an attractive girl who came from the other school. A custom at that time was for such friends to share an item, so she gave me her ring to wear. One day I lost the ring, and it was about that same time when a trusted friend came and told me that she was not a good girl. I was in deep trouble, and my conscience let me know it very well! For several days I was a walking prayer. I remember swishing the grass in our front yard with my shoe and asking, "What is faith?" I knew the Bible said that with faith we can move mountains, and I needed help!

In our trials, we had better ask God for His solution! "Be careful for nothing; but in every thing [commit your concerns] by prayer and supplication with thanksgiving let your [specific] requests be made known unto God. And the peace of God, which passeth all understanding [that transcends human explanation], shall keep your hearts [emotional stability] and minds [clear thinking] through [in] Christ Jesus" (Philippians 4:6-7).

I shared my concern with trusted friends, including a boy who lived on a farm near town. It was a fun place to be, and I remember being intrigued by his grandparents who only spoke the Dutch language.

About three weeks later, this friend came to me with the ring. What a relief! He had found it in the barnyard where the ground had been trodden by livestock. It was foolish of me to have had that ring in the first place, but God did teach me a lesson concerning the power of prayer. When I returned the ring to the girl she said, with a grin, that she had heard I had lost the ring and wanted to return it.

God's pattern for prayer in times of crisis is the biblical lamentation. The lament of the deeply troubled includes the following:
1. A plea to God: "Hear my cry, Oh God; I need Your help."
2. A reason for this prayer beyond the expression of distress is to share one's complaint to God in detail.
3. A plea for a specific remedy or, if He deems better, an entirely different plan of God's own design for meeting the need.
4. Commitment of trust: "I know You are there, Lord. I trust You. I believe You. I know You will help me in Your timing through this great crisis.
5. Assurance to yourself and to God that He is worthy of praise: "You, dear God, are worthy of unending praise."

One can find these elements in Christ's prayer at Calvary and in many of the Psalms, including Psalms 22, 51, and 74. The one through Whom we pray, the Lord Jesus Christ, suffered far greater than any other person could ever suffer, and it is the God Who raised Christ from the dead Who answers our prayers. Faith that turns our mind to the biblical lament protects us from unbelief, which is more harmful than any woundedness we can ever experience.

Dennis Reiter, an experienced counselor, called the importance of the biblical lament to this writer's attention. He suggests that we pray the prayer of lament for and with those who are so wounded they cannot think clearly.

"Rejoice evermore. Pray without ceasing. In every thing give thanks: for this is the will of God in Christ Jesus concerning you. Quench not the Spirit [keep self off the throne]. Despise not prophesyings [Bible predictions]. Prove all things [be responsible]; hold fast that which is good. Abstain from all appearance of evil [be patient; WAIT on God to do things in His way and on His time schedule]" (I Thessalonians 5:16-22).

To improve our prayer life, we need to know what prevents our prayers from being heard:

• Failure to pray in the name of Christ; it is Christ's death on the cross that gives those who have invited Christ into their life access to God. Christ's advocacy does not diminish the importance of consciously realizing that we are petitioning the Holy God of Creation. Expressing praise and adoration of God in worship opens the door to a proper prayer attitude.

Christ Himself said of God the Father, ". . . Hallowed be thy name" (Luke 11:2a). "Having therefore, brethren, boldness to enter into the holiest by the blood of Jesus" (Hebrews 10:19).

• It is unwise to pray for things that are inconsistent with the will of God. To do so would be asking for something that God cannot grant because it would be harmful. "And this is the confidence that we have in him, that, if we ask any thing according to his will, he heareth us" (I John 5:14). We find God's will by reading and meditating on His Word.

• It is fruitless to pray with motives that are self-centered. What is best is God's will, and it is important that God receive the glory for the victories He grants. "Herein is my Father glorified, that ye bear much fruit," (John 15:8a). "Ye ask, and receive not, because ye ask amiss, that ye may consume it upon your lusts" (James 4:3).

Acknowledge the hurts and face them head-on. It is important that we remove our guard and ask God to unmask any stumbling blocks that are in the way. "If the Son therefore shall make you free [place your burdens at the foot of the cross], ye shall be free indeed" (John 8:36).

• We cannot expect help when we pray as though God were not reliable. "If any of you lack wisdom, let him ask of God, that giveth to all men liberally, and upbraideth not; and it shall be given him. But let him ask in faith, nothing wavering. For he that wavereth is like a wave of the sea driven with the wind and tossed" (James 1:5-6).

• God cannot honor our prayers when we are living in sin. Sin, like a break in an electric circuit, cuts off the power. Emotions such as anger, bitterness, envy, jealousy and failure to ask forgiveness separate us from God's blessing and the insight essential for success. "Behold, the LORD'S hand is not shortened, that it cannot save; neither his ear heavy, that it cannot hear: But your iniquities have separated between you and your God, and your sins have hid his face from you, that he will not hear" (Isaiah 59:1-2).

"For he that eateth and drinketh unworthily [thinking condescendingly toward another], eateth and drinketh damnation to himself, not discerning the Lord's body [gift of God's grace purchased for all]. For this cause many are weak and sickly among you, and many sleep [die prematurely]" (I Corinthians 11:29-30).

"Search me, O God, and know my heart: try me, and know my thoughts: And see if there be any wicked way in me, and lead me in the way everlasting" (Psalm 139:23-24). "If we confess our sins, he is faithful and just to forgive us our sins, and to cleanse us from all unrighteousness" (I John 1:9).

• When praying with an unforgiving spirit, our prayers cannot be answered. "And when ye stand praying, forgive, if ye have ought against any: that your Father also which is in heaven may forgive you your trespasses" (Mark 11:25). I once observed an interview with the daughter of a couple who had been slain by white supremacists in the 1940s. She was asked if she was bitter toward the murderers. She had been well-taught by someone, perhaps her father. Paraphrased, her answer was, "No, I would not destroy myself by harboring bitterness and unforgiveness. That is for God to handle."

• We cannot expect God to hear our prayers when we are not thankful for His will in our life. "Because that, when they knew God, they glorified him not as God, neither were thankful; but became vain in their imaginations, and their foolish heart was darkened" (Romans 1:21).

• Unkindness between husband and wife can hinder prayer. If we find that we are treating others better than we treat our spouse, we are in trouble with God. The marriage relationship is second in importance only to our relationship with God. Even if the husband is a Bible reader and soul-winner, if he does not lead with patience and kindness, his prayers ring hollow.

"Likewise, ye husbands, dwell with them according to knowledge, giving honor [treat with respect] unto the wife, as unto the weaker vessel, and as being heirs together of the grace of life; that your prayers be not hindered" (I Peter 3:7). "Husbands, love your wives, even as Christ also loved the church, and gave himself [His life] for it" (Ephesians 5:25).

"And this is the confidence that we have in him, that, if we ask any thing according to his will [we determine God's will through prayer and reading His Word], he heareth us: And if we know that he hear us, whatsoever we ask, we know that we have the petitions that we desired of him" (I John 5:14-15).

Chapter Six

How to Listen to God

Have not I commanded thee? Be strong and of a good courage;
be not afraid, neither be thou dismayed: for the LORD thy God
is with thee whithersoever thou goest. Joshua 1:9

Are we listening to God? There is one basic reason why Christians falter (become unsteady in purpose and direction). **The reason God's people falter is that they do not listen to Him and proceed according to His instructions.**

Underlying our failure to listen to God are two factors:
1. We fail to understand that ever since the fall of man recorded in Genesis, mankind has been inundated with delusions of truth. As a consequence of man's rejection of God and Satan's intrusion, what seems right to us is NOT reliable!

"For they that are after the flesh [values of the world] do mind the things of the flesh; but they that are after the Spirit [lean not upon their own understanding, but upon] the things of the Spirit [God's revelation]. For to be carnally minded is death; but to be spiritually minded is life and peace" (Romans 8:5-6).

2. When we get hit by calamity, we tend to think we are ruined. **That is not true!**

[43]

Satan's trick is to fill us with deceptive emotions (feelings), generated by our old nature, to destroy our faith and to get us to rely upon the world.

The battle of overcoming the problems associated with quality goals is God's, not ours: "But rather seek ye the kingdom of God [truth and spiritual power]; and all these things shall be added unto you" (Luke 12:31).

"And we know that all things work together for good to them that love God, to them who are the called according to his purpose" (Romans 8:28).

Walking By Faith: Is faith unrealistic? Far from it. Faith in the living God brings us in touch with reality. Faith is an invisible support system that provides insight and strength to face and overcome visible problems.

Christians do not need to follow the world and their gullible nature. God's revelation is truth and His providence is sure! Listening to God provides us with the truth concerning potential outcomes and thus enables us to anticipate the short and long-term consequences of the choices at hand and, therefore, to make wise decisions.

Walking by faith can be illustrated by a little girl who, when walking on an icy sidewalk with her daddy, reaches up and takes his hand. We cannot see God with our eyes, but when we proceed by faith and act according to His instruction, we are, in effect, taking God's hand.

"He [Abraham] staggered not at the promise of God through unbelief; but was strong in faith, giving glory to God; And being fully persuaded that, what he [God] had promised, he was able also to perform. And therefore it was imputed to him [Abraham] for righteousness. Now it was not written for his sake alone, that it was imputed to him; But for us also, to whom it shall be imputed, if we believe on him [God] that raised up Jesus our Lord from the dead" (Romans 4:20-24).

God speaks to us in several ways. Unlike the misleading message of the world, His instruction is always reliable.

PRAYER: God speaks to those who ask for help. If we do not have God-honoring goals, if we are not sensitive enough to know what our needs are, then our ears and eyes for God are unemployed. A specific to-do list and prayer list work together. This list should be re-prioritized as problems are solved and God will continue to give victory over the challenges which confront us. "And whatsoever we ask [that is righteous and just], we receive of him, because we keep his commandments, and do those things that are pleasing in his sight" (I John 3:22).

Quite often God's timing for answers to prayer is not ours. Continue to search and acknowledge the need but do not give up. Our prayer should be "Lord, You solve this in Your time and in Your way—period."

Christ said, "Ask, and it shall be given you; seek, and ye shall find; knock, and it shall be opened unto you: For every one that asketh receiveth; and he that seeketh findeth; and to him that knocketh it shall be opened" (Matthew 7:7-8).

THE BIBLE: First and foremost, God speaks to us through His Word. "Thy word is a lamp unto my feet, and a light unto my path" (Psalms 119:105). The Bible is prominent in this book because it is God's Word that liberates us from woundedness. Helping those who are suffering emotional pain and in a state of woundedness is usually beyond the reach of our understanding. What is needed for healing is a search within the soul by and through God's Word.

Recognize that God's Word is true and practical in all matters:

Storing truth in our minds is the fundamental key to success. Study God's Word and ask Him for wisdom. The principal point is expressed in Proverbs.

Proverbs 2:1a: "My son, if thou wilt receive my words . . ." Receiving God's Word means getting the truth engrafted into one's values library (habit and attitude response resource).

Dependence upon God's Word gives understanding: "He keepeth the paths of judgment, and preserveth the way of his saints. Then shalt thou understand righteousness, and judgment [consequences of options available], and equity; yea, every good path" (Proverbs 2:8-9)." "O how I love thy law [truth about reality]! it is my meditation all the day. Thou through thy commandments hast made me wiser than mine enemies [the ways of Satan and his workers]: for they [God's words] are ever with me. I understand more than the ancients, because I keep thy precepts" (Psalms 119:97-98, 100).

"Thou shalt meditate therein day and night, that thou mayest observe to do according to all that is written therein: for then thou shalt make thy way prosperous, and then thou shalt have good success. Have not I commanded thee? Be strong and of a good courage; be not afraid, neither be thou dismayed: for the LORD thy God is with thee whithersoever thou goest" (Joshua 1:8b-9).

CIRCUMSTANCES AND EVENTS: God speaks to us through events and circumstances: "Quench not the Spirit. Despise not prophesyings. Prove all things (try what God says to do, and you will find that God is faithful); hold fast that which is good" (I Thessalonians 5:19-21).

We grow spiritually when we respond to God's Spirit by rejecting our self-centered nature which seeks to be the boss. "Abide in me, and I in you. As the branch cannot bear fruit of itself, except it abide in the vine; no more can ye, except ye abide in me" (John 15:4).

PEOPLE: God speaks to us through people **who trust Him and identify closely with His Word**. Our spouses are often our best advisors. We all have blind spots and do not need to be embarrassed by unintended mistakes. To be told in private about our shortcomings is of inestimable value.

SORROW: God did not create us to handle crises such as the death of a loved one or divorce, for these events could not have occurred prior to man's fall. When we become broken by losses that are too heavy to bear, God comes into our lives and helps us shoulder the burden. We learn more about trusting Him and our faith becomes stronger.

"Be content with such things as ye have: for he hath said, I will never leave thee, nor forsake thee. So that we may boldly say, The Lord is my helper, and I will not fear what man shall do unto me" (Hebrews 13:5b-6).

THE HOLY SPIRIT AND THE SPIRITUAL DIMENSION OF MAN: "And God said, Let us [Father, Son and Holy Spirit] make man in our image, after our likeness . . ." (Genesis 1:26a).

Except for the Holy Spirit, the unsaved would not see the depth of their sin and the need to receive Christ as their personal Lord and Savior. The Holy Spirit confirms the meaning of Scripture and teaches the saved how to feel about matters (to be emotionally mature). The human spirit could be described as a receiver that God uses to enter, enlighten, and empower the soul.

"Know ye not that ye [believers] are the temple of God, and that the Spirit of God dwelleth in you?" (I Corinthians 3:16). "Therefore if any man be in Christ, he is a new creature: old things are passed away [set aside]; behold, all things are become new" (II Corinthians 5:17).

In total contrast to our old nature, the Holy Spirit enlightens and empowers us to behave in a principled and enduring way. "That ye put off concerning the former conversation the old man, which is corrupt according to the deceitful lusts [sin-laden emotions]; And be renewed in the spirit of your mind; And that ye put on the new man, which after God is created in righteousness and true holiness [able to see evil and good for what they really are]" (Ephesians 4:22-24).

Satan also has a spiritual dimension and gains a deceptive advantage in our minds when we put God in second place. "Beloved, believe not every spirit, but try the spirits whether they are of God: because many false prophets are gone out into the world" (I John 4:1).

When walking with Christ (not self) on the throne, Christians can discern evil with their spirit and reject that evil without having to experience it and be defiled by it. God says, "I would have you wise unto that which is good, and simple [not involved] concerning evil" (Romans 16:19b).

CHURCH FELLOWSHIP: God speaks to us through membership in a Bible-believing church. Those who are active in a God-honoring church are strengthened and renewed because they become the beneficiaries of spiritual food, Scripture, prayer, meditation, song and fellowship. "And let us consider one another to provoke unto love and to good works" (Hebrews 10:24).

"And when they were come, and had gathered the church together, they rehearsed all that God had done with them, and how he had opened the door of faith unto the Gentiles" (Acts 14:27).

For the Christian, having Christ available to lead is already an accomplished fact. The only way we can miss out on God's leadership is to put self back on the throne. "**Peace I leave with you, my peace I give unto you**: not as the world giveth, give I unto you. Let not your heart be troubled, neither let it be afraid" (John 14:27).

Chapter Seven

The Most Powerful Force in Human Affairs

Beloved, let us love one another:
for love is of God; and every one that loveth is born
of God, and knoweth God. He that loveth not
knoweth not God; for God is love. I John 4:7-8

When we are spiritual, God's machinery is in place, our emotions are kept in abeyance, and problems remain manageable.

The gift of God's love in our lives, when directed toward others, is the greatest single remedy for problem relationships. Love is the light of the Holy Spirit through which the eyes of hurting people are opened to God.

Justice is the standard for treating others properly. Love is the manner of God's righteousness that reaches beyond justice. **Agape love** is the selfless devotion to God that causes one to have a forgiving and unselfish attitude toward others.

"And hope maketh not ashamed; because the love of God is shed abroad [present tense] in our hearts by the Holy Ghost which is given unto us," Romans 5:5. When Christ is Lord in our lives, His I Corinthians 13 provision protects our mind from Satan and from evil imaginations.

> Sadly, people can receive years of Bible training and never come to the point where Christ is the Lord in their life. They fail to realize that the indwelling patience and love of Christ are the essence of Christian character.

	Fruit of God's Spirit (Grace) Emotions Secure in God's Care	Fruit of Carnality (Pride) Emotions Uncontrolled
I Corinthians 13:		
Love suffereth long	Patient	Inconsiderate
And is kind	Goodwill	Mean spirited
Love envieth not	Content	Resentful
Love vaunteth not itself, is not puffed up	Humble	High-minded
Doth not behave itself unseemly	Courteous	Rude / imposing
Seeketh not her own	Secure in God	Must prevail
Is not easily provoked	Calm	Agitated
Thinketh no evil	Humbly focusing upon the good in other people	Desiring to judge, supported by evil imaginations
Rejoiceth not in iniquity, but rejoiceth in the truth	At peace, trusting God for the result	Self-righteous, desiring to expose the sin of others

The basis for emotional maturity and trouble-free relationships is having Christ in control. "In this was manifested the love of God toward us, because that God sent his only begotten Son into the world, that we might live through him. Herein is love, not that we loved God, but that he loved us, and sent his Son to be the propitiation for our sins. Beloved, if God so loved us, we ought also to love [live I Corinthians 13 toward] one another" (I John 4:9-11).

"And he [God] said unto me, My grace [power to forgive, love and be patient] is [present tense] sufficient for thee: for my strength is made perfect in weakness . . ." (II Corinthians 12:9). "Finally, brethren, farewell. Be perfect, be of good comfort, be of one mind, live in peace; and the God of love and peace shall be with you" (II Corinthians 13:11).

"Humble yourselves in the sight of the Lord, and he shall lift you up. Speak not evil one of another, brethren . . . There is one lawgiver, who is able to save and to destroy: who art thou [to act as though you are God] that judgest another? Therefore to him that knoweth to do good [I Corinthians 13], and doeth it not, to him it is sin" (James 4:10-12, 17).

Trusting God for Outcomes Is Always Best:
• When we trust God to be the Judge, our emotions will be at peace and under control. Issues may remain issues, but this should not prevent us from showing God's love to those who offend. They may be hurting, or they may be responding wrongly and need to be restored, but from the perspective of our emotions we will not take the offense personally.

• When we make issues out of people rather than the behavior that calls for correction, the issue gets clouded. The problem becomes more difficult to isolate in the minds of the participants. "But strong meat belongeth to them that are of full age, even those who by reason of use have their senses exercised [Spirit-controlled] to discern both good and evil" (Hebrews 5:14).

• Keeping calm (remaining courteous) and separating from troublemakers, if necessary, eliminates a distraction that might otherwise deter the sinner from seeing his own sin. "But I say unto you, Love your enemies, bless them that curse you, do good to them that hate you, and pray for them which despitefully use you, and persecute you" (Matthew 5:44).

• Unkindness toward others complicates any solution. They may not understand our complaint because of the distortion that tends to accompany emotionally-charged complaints. "And beside this, giving all diligence, add to your faith virtue; and to virtue knowledge; And to knowledge temperance; and to temperance patience; and to patience godliness; And to godliness brotherly kindness; and to brotherly kindness charity. For if these things be in you, and abound, they make you that ye shall neither be barren nor unfruitful in the knowledge of our Lord Jesus Christ" (II Peter 1:5-8).

• When we are emotionally upset with a person, our mindset will not let us take advice from that individual. The possibility exists that the offender's estimation of the situation is better than our own. Then, when God imposes the judgment of truth upon us, we find out the hard way that the other person was right. "Looking diligently lest any man fail [fall short] of the grace of God; lest any root of bitterness springing up trouble you, and thereby many be defiled" (Hebrews 12:15).

• In marriage, child/parent, employee/employer and important organization relationships, persistent and uncontrolled emotions can force a painful and heartbreaking separation. "For, brethren, ye have been called unto liberty; only use not liberty for an occasion to the flesh, but by love serve one another. But if ye bite and devour one another, take heed that ye be not consumed one of another" (Galatians 5:13, 15).

• The absence of charity (love) causes people to strike out with gossip. If the gossip is rejected by the hearer, then the only damage done is the exposure of our own spiritual immaturity. If, however, the hearer accepts the poison of our gossip, his mind may become defiled.

"A good man out of the good treasure of his heart bringeth forth that which is good; and an evil man out of the evil treasure of his heart bringeth forth that which is evil: for of the abundance of the heart his mouth speaketh" (Luke 6:45).

> The most powerful force in human relations is the God-given power to love the unlovable. In order for this love to be removed from the attitude of a Christian, he or she must put self back on the throne as the boss!

"But the fruit of the Spirit is love, joy, peace, longsuffering, gentleness, goodness, faith, Meekness, temperance: against such there is no law. Brethren, if a man be overtaken in a fault, ye which are spiritual, restore such an one in the spirit of meekness; considering thyself, lest thou also be tempted. Bear ye one another's burdens, and so fulfil the law of Christ" (Galatians 5:22-23; 6:1-2).

God's way provides emotional balance and peace. "Be not wise in thine own eyes: fear the LORD [be selfless and humble] and [thusly] depart from evil [driven emotions]. It shall be health to thy navel, and marrow to thy bones" (Proverbs 3:7-8).

Chapter Eight

Our Soul, the Personality of Man

And the very God of peace sanctify [empower] you
wholly [for upright living]; and I pray God your whole spirit
and SOUL and body be preserved blameless unto the
coming of our Lord Jesus Christ. I Thessalonians 5:23

In this chapter we will review the agencies we use to superintend emotions and make balanced decisions. The mind and spirit are identified by what they do, but in ways beyond our understanding they overlap and function together. They proceed like members of an orchestra who, when working together, provide beautiful music. As individuals we are responsible for the functions of our minds and the spiritual values our decisions project.

THE SOUL: The condition of our soul (mind, will, and emotion) is a primary concern to God. "For ye were as sheep going astray; but are now returned unto the Shepherd [watchful guide] and Bishop [unerring Authority] of your souls" (I Peter 2:25). The soul and spirit of man are distinguishable from one another. Man's spirit could be described as a receiver that God uses to enlighten and even empower our soul for righteousness.

"Now we [those who have accepted Christ] have received, not the spirit of the world, but the spirit which is of God [truth]; that we might know the things [discern good from bad] that are freely given to us of God" (I Corinthians 2:12).

Our personality is a reflection of the values we adopt (that become rooted in the soul). The development and uniqueness of the soul are the real you! Immeasurably better than the best computers, the mental function of the soul includes assembling information and making choices. To function properly, the soul must be free from sin that emanates from the outside, and it must be free from subjective sin, prejudices, and evil imaginations that are generated from within.

When we are honoring God, we find that our emotions remain in subjection and our decisions are greatly improved. The following diagrams reflect the three conditions of man in this life:

This person quite naturally has self or ego (E) on the throne. He remains separated from God. He is spiritually dead because Christ, who gives purpose and insight, has been rejected from his life.

This person repented and invited Christ (†) into his life as Lord and Savior from sin, but he then puts self (E) back on the throne as the boss over decisions.

Here we have the picture of a born-again Christian who remains humble and trusts his or her decisions to Christ's influence. Peace, discernment, and victory as a new person in Christ become a reality.

For those who are walking in Christ, the ability of their mind to assess reality without prejudice and to set priorities is phenomenal. The book of Hebrews often speaks of the "heart" as the place where decisions are formed: "Keep thy heart with all diligence; for out of it are the issues of life" (Proverbs 4:23).

"Beware lest any man spoil you through philosophy and vain deceit, after the tradition of men, after the rudiments of the world, and not after Christ [truth]" (Colossians 2:8). "For as the body without the spirit [of God working] is dead [spiritually], so faith without works [God-honoring activity] is dead also" (James 2:26).

The soul is also likened to the inner man. The stronger the inner man, the weaker flesh is in stirring up wickedness. "That he would grant you, according to the riches of his glory, to be strengthened with might by his Spirit in the inner man; That Christ may dwell in your hearts by faith; that ye, being rooted and grounded in love, May be able to comprehend with all saints what is the breadth, and length, and depth, and height; And to know the love of Christ, which passeth knowledge, that ye might be filled with all the fulness of God" (Ephesians 3:16-19).

OUR CONSCIOUS MIND: Reasoning is the capacity of the mind to assimilate evidence and determine the best course of action necessary to remedy a given situation.

The human will to act comes in response to rational choices or reactions to our emotions. Our actions will either be consistent with the values consciously adopted in the past (stored in our memory bank) or will follow subjective emotions.

Examples of reasoning that flows from disrespect for, and ignorance of God's Word:

Rationalization — coming to conclusions in the absence of revealed truth (God's Word) which leave one under the influence of the world's prejudices and values (Genesis 3:6; Jeremiah 17:9; Romans 1:21; II Corinthians 11:14; II Timothy 3:7).

Idealization — unrealistic assessment that leaves a person blindsided to realities and leads to unintended consequence (Romans 1:22-23; II Corinthians 10:12).

Mysticism — religious fixation on dreamy and groundless perceptions of reality that detract from the search for truth found in the Bible (Romans 1:21; II Corinthians 10:5).

Displacement — a defense mechanism of avoiding problems that need to be acknowledged by shifting the problems to others (Psalm 52:3; Hebrews 4:13).

Projection — attributing one's own attitudes, feelings, or desires to someone else as a defense against guilt and anxiety (Psalm 36:2-4; Proverbs 20:17; Luke 18:14b).

SUBCONSCIOUS MIND: The subconscious mind is our values library. It is the library that stores the interpretations we consciously place on observations. This library is not a discriminating agency. **It takes what we give it. In other words, we cannot secretly harbor sinful thoughts without having them stored in our library and eventually becoming a part of us.** The more a value is stored, the more controlling it becomes. "For where your treasure is [what you interpret to be desirable], there will your heart [attitudes and goals] be also" (Matthew 6:21).

When we persist in consciously interpreting observations according to Scriptural standards, a desirable influence (habit base) for future decisions accumulates in our subconscious library.

"Be not deceived; God is not mocked: for whatsoever a man soweth [be it good or evil], that shall he also reap. For he that soweth to his flesh shall of the flesh reap corruption; but he that soweth to the Spirit [according to God's Word] shall of the Spirit reap life everlasting" (Galatians 6:7-8).

"Thy word have I hid in mine heart, that I might not sin against thee" (Psalm 119:11). This process of learning and adopting God's values for life is called sanctification. With Scripture as the mind's foundation for our decisions, success comes more readily, and our faith is strengthened.

"But his delight is in the law of the LORD; and in his law doth he meditate day and night. And he shall be like a tree planted by the rivers of water, that bringeth forth his fruit in his season; his leaf also shall not wither; and whatsoever he doeth shall prosper" (Psalm 1:2-3).

How long does it take for the new value, consciously applied and stored in our subconscious library, to dominate and replace the old value base for decisions? It varies, but how long does it take to learn to follow the script for the piano before good piano music flows automatically? How much time is required before we learn to ride a bicycle?

I served two years in the Army as a dental technician, and during that time my wife and I befriended a dental assistant, Richard Carpenter, and his wife. They had several children and could not afford an automobile, so we took them to church and to purchase groceries. For almost a year he would constantly ask, "Dave, do you think I could be a dentist?" So I helped him evaluate the idea, and I advised him that he could succeed. He could attend the first four years of college on the GI Bill. He could then go on to dental school if his wife worked at night while he stayed home in the evenings to care for the children.

Near the end of this period, a startling change of mind overcame me. Originally my goal had been to farm, which I had learned to do while living with a farm family. Beyond that, I was very negative about academics. My first grade teacher had let it be known that she thought I was ignorant, and she would embarrass me in front of the other students. It was my dubious privilege to spend two years in her first grade class! When I was a little older, I responded to an ad for children to go door-to-door selling small containers of salve to neighbors. That was a frightening experience. When standing for the high school graduation picture, I assured a friend of two things: "I will never go to college, and I will never be a salesman!"

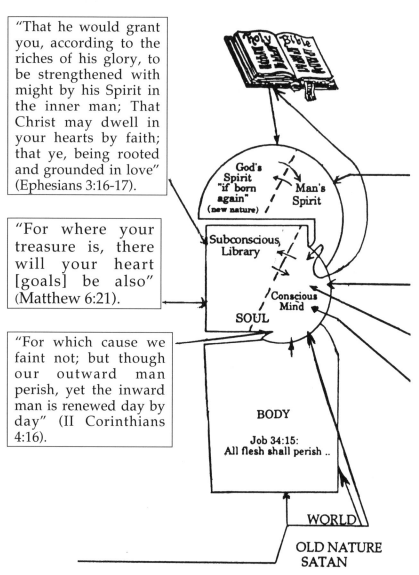

"That he would grant you, according to the riches of his glory, to be strengthened with might by his Spirit in the inner man; That Christ may dwell in your hearts by faith; that ye, being rooted and grounded in love" (Ephesians 3:16-17).

"For where your treasure is, there will your heart [goals] be also" (Matthew 6:21).

"For which cause we faint not; but though our outward man perish, yet the inward man is renewed day by day" (II Corinthians 4:16).

God's Spirit "if born again" (new nature)

Man's Spirit

Subconscious Library

Conscious Mind

SOUL

BODY

Job 34:15: All flesh shall perish ..

WORLD

OLD NATURE SATAN

Their goal is to deceivingly make evil look good, pleasant, and desirable. Their purpose is to activate the old nature, destroy the Christian, and ruin God's reputation.

SANCTIFICATION — "And the very God of peace sanctify you wholly; and I pray God your whole SPIRIT and SOUL and BODY be preserved blameless unto the coming of our Lord Jesus Christ" (I Thessalonians 5:23).

"But his delight is in the law of the LORD; and in his law doth he meditate day and night. And he shall be like a tree planted by the rivers of water, that bringeth forth his fruit in his season; his leaf also shall not wither; and whatsoever he doeth shall prosper" (Psalm 1:2-3).

"And be not conformed to this world: but be ye transformed by the renewing of your mind, that ye may prove what is that good, and acceptable, and perfect, will of God" (Romans 12:2).

"Casting down imaginations, and every high thing that exalteth itself against the knowledge of God, and bringing into captivity every thought to the obedience of Christ" (II Corinthians 10:5).

"Finally, brethren, whatsoever things are true, whatsoever things are honest, whatsoever things are just, whatsoever things are pure, whatsoever things are lovely, whatsoever things are of good report; if there be any virtue, and if there be any praise, think on these things" (Philippians 4:8).

The startling change of mind that came over me was, "I can go to college, and I should go to college!" This was a complete reversal of my belief on that subject. While helping my friend evaluate his prospects for becoming a dentist, I was unknowingly storing new and better values in my own mind's library. This experience could be spelled out in more detail, but the sum of it is this: An interpretation (good or evil) placed upon one's observations, over time is stored in one's values library and becomes a very powerful force over one's life!

It took me a few months to learn how to study, but by the grace of God I received a four-year degree with honors in three years. Ironically, the business success I experienced later was based upon training salespeople. My friend, a poor Arkansas sharecropper's son, went on to become a successful dentist. This process of storing values and how it relates to overall success is covered in chapter twelve.

After studying the preceding illustration, what do you find to be missing? When an evil interpretation is adopted and enters into our mind's library, what is our first line of attack in order to clean up our values base? "If we confess [repent and turn away from] our sins, he [God] is faithful and just to forgive us our sins, and to cleanse us from all unrighteousness" (I John 1:9).

THE HUMAN WILL: We are responsible for the consequences that result from rejecting God's will. The flesh is always present, desiring to control our will. The choice between trusting self or trusting God is the final link in the decision-making chain that precipitates action. "There is therefore now no condemnation to them which are in Christ Jesus, who walk not after the flesh, but after the Spirit" (Romans 8:1).

"This is a faithful saying, and these things I will that thou affirm constantly, that they which have believed in God might be careful to maintain good works. These things are good and profitable unto men" (Titus 3:8).

THE FLESH: Sometimes the Bible uses the word *flesh* for "sin nature." Other times, the word *flesh* refers to the source of sin-laden feelings or emotions. It is the superintending of the Holy Spirit along with conscious evaluation, not emotional stimulus, that can assess the consequences of choices. Although emotions (feelings) can have an important role, judgment made on the basis of feelings apart from God's instruction is very dangerous.

CASTING DOWN IMAGINATIONS AND EMOTIONS THAT LEAD TO ILLUSON AND HARMFUL ACTION:

* "But if the Spirit of him that raised up Jesus from the dead dwell in you, he that raised up Christ from the dead shall also quicken your mortal bodies [empowered to overcome evil and do good] by his Spirit that dwelleth in you" (Romans 8:11).
* "But the fruit of the Spirit is love, joy, peace, longsuffering, gentleness, goodness, faith, Meekness, temperance: against such there is no law. And they that are Christ's have crucified the flesh with the affections and lusts [evil-laden emotions]" (Galatians 5:22-24).
* "For as many as are led by the Spirit of God, they are the sons of God. For ye have not received the spirit of bondage again to fear [entrapment by sinful imaginations and emotions]; but ye [God's children] have received the Spirit of adoption, whereby we cry, Abba, Father" (Romans 8:14-15).
* "That whosoever looketh on a woman to lust after her hath committed adultery with her already in his heart" (Matthew 5:28b). "Casting down imaginations [illusions, fantasies, mysticism], and every high thing that exalteth itself against the knowledge of God, and bringing into captivity every thought [displace wasteful and evil imaginations with biblical realities] to the obedience of Christ" (II Corinthians 10:5).
* "I beseech you therefore, brethren, by the mercies of God, that ye present your bodies a living sacrifice, holy, acceptable unto God, which is your reasonable service. And be not conformed to this world: but be ye transformed by the renewing of your mind, that ye may

prove what is that good, and acceptable, and perfect, will of God [be a visible demonstration of God's goodness and power]" (Romans 12:1-2).

- "But they that wait upon the LORD shall renew their strength; they shall mount up with wings as eagles . . ." (Isaiah 40:31).

OUR CONSCIENCE, HONESTY, AND WISE DECISIONS: A healthy conscience serves as a guide by sending out an alarm when we go wrong. "Know ye not that ye are the temple of God, and that the Spirit of God dwelleth in you?" (I Corinthians 3:16). In other words, truth is revealed by God's Spirit to our spirit which, in turn, prompts us through the voice of our conscience. "But strong meat belongeth to them that . . . have their senses exercised to discern both good and evil" (Hebrews 5:14). "Blessed is he whose transgression is forgiven, whose sin is covered" (Psalm 32:1).

Dishonesty undermines the conscience in its ability to support good decisions. "This charge I commit unto thee, son Timothy . . . that thou by them mightest war a good warfare; Holding faith, and a good conscience; which some having put away concerning faith have made shipwreck" (I Timothy 1:18-19).

The secularization of public schools is obviously tailored to wreck the consciences of students. People wanting to know why there is so much violence among youth need look no further than public education. "Unto the pure all things are pure: but unto them that are defiled and unbelieving is nothing pure; but even their mind and conscience is defiled" (Titus 1:15). "He that covereth his sins shall not prosper: but whoso confesseth and forsaketh them shall have mercy" (Proverbs 28:13).

Doing things contrary to our conscience fouls up relationships at three levels.

First, having a clear conscience is essential to the work of the indwelling Holy Spirit. Untruthfulness is a sin against our own spirit and a rejection of God. "Perverseness therein is a breach in the spirit" (Proverbs 15:4b). Returning in our mind to God's standard of right and confessing our guilt to Him clears our conscience with God. "How much more shall the blood of Christ, who through the eternal Spirit offered himself without spot to God, purge your conscience from dead works to serve the living God?" (Hebrews 9:14).

Second, maintaining a clear conscience is essential for the health of our own soul. "Neither give heed to fables and endless genealogies, which minister questions [sin-laden emotions and deviant imaginations], rather than godly edifying which is in faith [in God's Word]: so do. Now the end of the commandment is charity out of a pure heart, and of a good conscience, and of faith unfeigned" (I Timothy 1:4-5). "Wherefore lay apart all filthiness and superfluity of naughtiness [harmful to relationships], and receive with meekness the engrafted word, which is able to save your souls [mind, will, and emotion]" (James 1:21).

Third, failure to have a clear conscience in our relationship with others undermines the basis for sustaining strong relationships. "For our rejoicing is this, the testimony of our conscience, that in simplicity and godly sincerity, not with fleshly wisdom, but by the grace of God, we have had our conversation [honest and gracious toward others] in the world, and more abundantly to you-ward" (II Corinthians 1:12).

It is very important that there be no unkindness in our heart toward God or man when partaking in communion! **"For he that eateth and drinketh unworthily, eateth and drinketh damnation to himself, not discerning the Lord's body. For this cause many are weak and sickly among you, and many sleep** [premature death]. For if we would judge ourselves, we should not be judged. But when we are judged, we are chastened of the Lord, that we should not be condemned with the world" (I Corinthians 11:29-32).

> Heartfelt respect and worship of almighty God as the only true Benefactor and a desire to do things according to His Word lead to blessings beyond measure.

THANKFULNESS AND HOPE ARE THE FRAME FOR LIFE'S DYNAMIC: Our love for God, thankfulness, and hope run together. Being unthankful suggests that we are not aware of and do not appreciate the benefit of God's care.

• "And let the peace of God rule in your hearts, to the which also ye are called in one body; and be ye thankful" (Colossians 3:15).

• "Let the word of Christ dwell in you richly in all wisdom; [which includes] teaching and admonishing one another in psalms and hymns and spiritual songs, singing with grace [thankfulness] in your hearts to the Lord" (Colossians 3:16).

• "Because that, when they knew God, they glorified him not as God, neither were thankful; but became vain in their imaginations, and [because they were unthankful] their foolish heart was darkened [reliable hope abandoned]" (Romans 1:21).

• "A merry heart [humor and thankfulness] doeth good like a medicine: but a broken spirit [loss of hope] drieth the bones" (Proverbs 17:22).

Guess who I just had for lunch?

Chapter Nine

Spiritual Woundedness

Restore unto me the joy of thy salvation;
and uphold me with thy free spirit. Psalm 51:12

Peace of mind and a feeling of wholeness occur when relationships are spiritually harmonious. Without God's help, wholeness in this sin-cursed world is impossible.

> The causes of woundedness are an offense to the goodness of creation. Consequently, God's intervention and time for healing are needed. Time is necessary for healing because we are mentally and spiritually slow in coming to Him.

Victimization by an injustice is often the cause of woundedness. The loss of a vital part of one's life—be it love, an individual, or whatever—can be disabling. If, however, we dedicate what we acquire to God, then the protection of our possessions, beyond the application of common sense on our part, rests with God!

It is not unreasonable to suggest that woundedness may also result from a deep-seated possessiveness held subconsciously that has not yet adopted the conscious will to give all to God. The key is knowing God's Word and resting in His overcoming power for peace and harmony of mind.

The disfunction of woundedness may be marginal, as with Peg in chapter four. Conversely, however, the breakdown in a wounded person's ability to think clearly may be so overwhelming that he or she needs intensive care.

For further insight into woundedness, I share the following experience. Many years ago, our company attorney informed me that a person on my staff was going around criticizing me. This upset me. I waited a couple days until I was able to give Christ priority on the throne of my mind and invited the man to my office. I confronted him with the remarks he had made to the attorney, stating, "I do make mistakes, but how will I know your opinion if you go around telling others and not me? What's the problem?" As it turned out, I had dismissed a secretary, and he was offended by what he perceived to be an unreasoned dismissal.

Both of us were wounded by what the other person had done. It was not deep-seated, but it illustrates spiritual woundedness. In the absence of grace, the woundedness short-circuited our capacity to think right. After finding out what I had done to offend him, I apologized without making any excuses, and he forgave me and was released from his woundedness.

In Review, What Would the Consequences Have Been if Healing Had Not Occurred?

1. Communications breakdown: Harmful emotions were aroused by the offense of the other person. Anger and the need to impose retribution came into our minds. One person gossiped. Socially we were driven apart and no

longer grateful for the contribution of the other person toward mutual goals. The separation could have been permanent. He could have quit, or I could have fired him. But in either case, both of our futures would have been harmed. "Looking diligently lest any man fail of the grace of God; lest any root of bitterness springing up trouble you, and thereby many be defiled" (Hebrews 12:15).

It was important that I had learned to distrust my emotions. I waited until the emotional self had yielded control to Christ before seeking reconciliation. This is what we mean by emotional maturity. "He hath shewed thee, O man, what is good; and what doth the LORD require of thee, but to do justly, and to love mercy, and to walk humbly with thy God?" (Micah 6:8).

2. Judgmentalism: We added to our woundedness by demanding standards for the other party that we ourselves could not meet. "Therefore thou art inexcusable, O man, whosoever thou art that judgest: for wherein thou judgest another, thou condemnest thyself; for thou that judgest doest the same things" (Romans 2:1).

3. An important relationship was being destroyed by untamed emotions; we may have even experienced some depression. "Even in laughter the heart is sorrowful; and the end of that mirth is heaviness" (Proverbs 14:13). "My soul is weary of my life; I will leave my complaint upon myself; I will speak in the bitterness of my soul" (Job 10:1).

4. Rebellion: All of this occurred because self, rather than Christ, was on the throne. We were in trouble with God. "For rebellion [rejection of our Creator's help] is as the sin of witchcraft, and stubbornness is as iniquity and idolatry. Because thou hast rejected the word of the LORD, he hath also rejected thee [cannot use you] from being king" (I Samuel 15:23).

When a person within a family, church, or another people-intensive setting becomes wounded, the experience can be exceedingly painful. It may take years for this woundedness to heal, if it ever does. Much patience by loved ones and friends is in order. A never-give-up, prayerful search for the answer which will unlock the woundedness is important.

Many years ago my father did something that was harmless, but it unleashed an emotional response of bitterness and anger within me. I was surprised and ashamed that such feelings, which had no justification, could persist inside me. It was not easy, but thankfully I kept the anger from erupting. There is room here for speculation about the cause, but I had consciously rejected any justification for the anger and yet it took three or four months for it to lift.

The book *Portrait of Obedience* describes the trauma of woundedness in the experience of a prominent pastor. Dr. Franklin (a fictitious name) was wounded in spirit when another Christian leader spread false criticisms concerning his daughter. She had served sacrificially as a missionary and had become very ill. As a believer, Franklin knew that the offense was God's problem, **but his emotions would not let him turn it over to God**. Finally, after many days of agitation and great personal torment, his mind reported, "Son, I know you can't (forgive this offensive man), but I (your God) can; and if you really want me to do it, I will do it through you." In that moment, Dr. Franklin grasped the sufficiency of God's grace. Before he knew what was happening, he was pouring out his heart in a passion of love for the offender and asking God to forgive his self-righteousness and straighten him [self] out. We know that Christ is on the throne when we experience love rather than bitterness toward an offender.

> Dr. Franklin's emotional balance was restored the moment he honestly confronted his own insufficiency and accepted the power of God's love to forgive. He knew that it was only God's love that enabled him to so pray.

Following are eight situations which, singly or in combination, are known for causing woundedness. Interestingly, they resemble the list of offenses toward God and man that make our prayers ineffective (chapter five).

GOSSIP: Gossip is one of the most common causes of emotional pain and ruined relationships. Gossip is making derogatory reports about a person in his or her absence. Making a derogatory remark about a person outside of the Matthew 18:15-17 pattern is exceedingly wicked. The jury members, verse 17, come from the group whose dynamic is endangered by the gossip.

The gossip of a carnal Christian and Dr. Franklin's permitting that gossip to enter and defile his mind were responsible for Dr. Franklin's woundedness. Gossip may walk in on the back of half-truth, but gossiping is a foolish assumption of knowledge and authority that belongs to God alone. We all make mistakes a thousand times over. For the sake of God's reputation, our mistakes are to be confronted personally according to Matthew 18:15. The spiritual growth of children is hindered when they hear adults gossiping. Satan promotes gossip through people who, for any number of reasons, wish to diminish the reputation of others. Gossip from a trusted sibling to another sibling about a parent can poison the spirit of an unsuspecting brother or sister against the parent.

Satan, the deceiver, becomes involved in gossip as an angel of light. We must not accept gossip. It will defile our minds and unleash harmful emotions. "And the tongue is a fire, a world of iniquity . . . it defileth the whole body . . . and it is set on fire of hell" (James 3:6).

"A wholesome tongue is a tree of life: but perverseness therein is a breach in the [one's own] spirit" (Proverbs 15:4). "A froward man soweth strife: and a whisperer separateth chief friends" (Proverbs 16:28).

All communications should enhance God's reputation. Gossip by persons who are looked up to and respected does the greatest harm.

"Let your light so shine before men, that they may see your good works, and glorify your Father which is in heaven" (Matthew 5:16). "Whatsoever things are lovely . . . of good report . . . if there be any virtue, and if there be any praise [use your mind to], think on these things" (Philippians 4:8b).

UNFORGIVING SPIRIT: Offenses should not be taken personally. To forgive is deciding not to be conflicted in one's emotions by the supposed right to punish the offender. The matter is left in God's hands. Christians who are continually causing conflict have received God's forgiveness, but they are denying that grace to others.

"For if ye forgive men their trespasses, your heavenly Father will also forgive you: But if ye forgive not men their trespasses, neither will your Father forgive your trespasses" (Matthew 6:14-15).

When we do not forgive another person, (1) our prayers become ineffective, (2) we grieve the Holy Spirit, (3) we wound ourselves emotionally, and (4) our minds support and intensify the extremes of our emotions.

Others need and deserve (because of the cross) my forgiveness just as I need and deserve (because of Christ's sacrifice) the forgiving mercy of others. In the absence of love as the controller of our emotions, Christ's sacrifice for relationships becomes of no effect. To forgive a person and to remember the good they have done is not compromise. Forgiveness was purchased by Christ on the cross.

JUDGMENTALISM: Judgmentalism differs from the sin of an unforgiving spirit. Judgmentalism grabs on to trouble by meddling in matters that are not our business in the first place. Judgmentalism and an unforgiving spirit ride on the backs of two different dispositions: one concerns things we observe in others that affect us while the other stands upon self-righteous imaginations.

We may need to separate from an offensive person on the basis of his behavior, but we have no right to assume God's authority to condemn or punish. Sometimes we may need to clarify our actions to another, but it is fruitless to try to defend oneself. God is our defender! The truth always manifests itself in time, and people with character will then realize who was right and who was wrong. I have seen this happen time and time again.

When listening to others, we tune in at one of two levels. One is pride and judgmentalism and the other is humility and remembering that they belong to God.

Playing "gotcha" is very harmful to one's emotional stability and to relationships. When a person persists in storing up condemnation toward another, it will eventually turn to uncontrollable bitterness and explode outwardly.

In order to rid ourselves of the "gotcha" mentality, we must become sensitive to the magnitude of our own sin. Confusion of mind always follows when we set standards for others that we ourselves cannot meet. Judging others is injurious not only to our own soul but also to our life expectancy.

"But let a man examine himself . . . For he that eateth and drinketh unworthily, eateth and drinketh damnation to himself, not discerning the Lord's body" (I Corinthians 11:28-29).

"Dearly beloved, avenge not yourselves, but rather give place unto wrath: for it is written, Vengeance is mine; I will repay, saith the Lord. Be not overcome of evil, but overcome evil with good" (Romans 12:19, 21).

"But when we are judged [found sinful and unrepentant], we are chastened of the Lord, that we should not be condemned with the world" (I Corinthians 11:32).

> "And thinkest thou this, O man, that judgest them which do such things, and doest the same, that thou shalt escape the judgment of God?" (Romans 2:3).

DISRESPECT FOR AUTHORITY: Being under authority is not being under control. It is being under God's protection. Respect for authorities is an emotional stabilizer. The help provided by authorities established in the Bible can be illustrated by the protective wall or "breakwater" that shields boats in a harbor from devastation.

Getting the boat into the harbor may be inconvenient because of the rock barrier, but the barrier tames the waves and keeps the boats safe. Similarly husbands, parents of youth, pastors, employers, police, and other officials may be an inconvenience at times, but they play an important role in our progress.

Failure to honor in one's heart God's established authorities may be traced to the very seat of our emotions. To speak evil of authorities is characteristic of apostasy (Jude 8). It is not wrong, however, to disagree with God's designated authority in matters of objective reality. We may appeal to them and ask what it is that they wish to accomplish and suggest alternatives. In limited instances, we may even need to separate from them, but it is very important that we do not dishonor them in our heart. When we become bitter toward authority figures, we are in trouble with God. "For rebellion [against God's authority] is as the sin of witchcraft, and stubbornness is as iniquity and idolatry" (I Samuel 15:23). Rebellion and witchcraft are terms that indicate a subjection to the realm of Satan.

God established the family, Bible-based churches, and government. Disrespect for authority leaves us blind-sided to realities that matter. Paul warned, "Whosoever therefore resisteth the power [authority], resisteth the ordinance of God: and they that resist shall receive to themselves damnation" (Romans 13:2). "Hear counsel, and receive instruction, that thou mayest be wise in thy latter end" (Proverbs 19:20).

Pastors: An example of a God-ordained authority figure is the church pastor. His ministry includes teaching God's Word to the people so they can escape the wiles of Satan.

He teaches them God's rules for fellowship and progress. In some instances, answers to questions confronted by a church do not clearly fit "Thus saith the Lord." The leader then challenges the people to pray for wisdom so they might move according to a Spirit-led consensus. An important role of pastors (as well as other leader authorities) is to serve as the focal point for the unity that is needed to maintain group dynamic. Pastors and leader servants such as husbands are accountable to God!

"And the servant of the Lord [leaders such as pastors] must not strive [continual aggression]; but be gentle unto all men, apt to teach, patient, In meekness instructing those that oppose themselves [deviate from God's Word]; if God peradventure will give them repentance to the acknowledging [full and complete] of the truth; And that they may recover themselves out of the snare of the devil, who are taken captive by him at his will" (II Timothy 2:24-26).

It is God who ultimately rules over individuals, families, churches, leaders, and nations. Pastor-leaders, for example, in churches which function like a miniature republic, serve at the will of the church membership led by God's Word and the Holy Spirit, and thus may be removed by God. If members get upset with the pastor, they can leave. Gossip against the pastor is rebellion against God. Failure to follow the Matthew 18:15-17 procedure destroys friendships and causes great organizational and emotional injury. The membership will recognize if the pastor or an elected government official becomes unqualified, and they, rather than a few spin-doctors or gossips, have the authority to remove the leader.

Employers: One of the greatest proofs of God's power is that he uses people who are sinners for meaningful helper roles. We honor employers for providing us with work and an income. We can appeal to an employer for change when work problems seem unmanageable, or sometimes we may need to change employment. It helps to remember that God is sovereign! We are actually working for God, not the employer. We are to work cheerfully and look to God for promotion.

"Servants, obey in all things your masters according to the flesh; not with eyeservice, as menpleasers [even when not being watched]; but in singleness of heart, fearing God: And whatsoever ye do, do it heartily, as to the Lord [in reality you are serving God], and not unto men; Knowing that of the Lord ye shall receive the reward of the inheritance [God's provision]: for ye serve the Lord Christ" (Colossians 3:22-24).

PARENT/CHILD RELATIONSHIPS: Dishonoring one's parents is a mistake that has serious emotional consequences. The command to "honour thy father and thy mother" is one of the Ten Commandments in Exodus 20. The verse goes on to say, "that thy days may be long upon the land which the LORD thy God giveth thee." God knows parents are human. We will not always agree with them, but we are to honor them as the ones whom God has used to give us life.

"Children, obey your parents in all things: for this [self-discipline and safety] is well pleasing unto the Lord. Fathers, provoke not your children to anger, lest they be discouraged" (Colossians 3:20-21).

As a child, I noticed strange behavior by a certain young man when he was around his father. However, the other siblings were normal. His grandmother saw this also. I asked her about the behavior, but she did not understand it either. I wonder now if this young man had gone through a period of self-righteousness that overpowered any respect he should have demonstrated toward his father. Whatever the problem was, it harmed his life.

The son's behavior would sometimes drive the dad to tears. On one occasion the son was filling the gas tank of a farm tractor while smoking. His father courteously expressed concern. The son rejected this advice and made it clear that embers from cigarettes do not ignite gas fumes. Fortunately, he did not blow them all up!

Many observed the public display of disrespect by Patti Davis toward her parents, Ronald and Nancy Reagan. In her writing she acknowledges being angry and living a very risky lifestyle. Patti's emotional state and blatant disrespect had to be very painful to her parents. In one of her books, Patti quoted her dad as saying, "What went wrong?" We do not know with exactness, but Scripture warns against dishonoring (in our mind) our parents.

"Whoso curseth his father or his mother, his lamp shall be put out in obscure darkness" (Proverbs 20:20). Mosaic Law for showing deference toward authority has a parallel to our attitudes such as humility, love, and grace, which have broader application than we may realize.

LOSS OF LOVE: Penned for us over 2,000 years ago, the Bible tells us that love, hope, and health are interrelated. The book, *The Broken Heart* by Dr. James Lynch of the John Hopkins Medical School, documents that truth. Dr. Lynch points out that "even the most elementary forms of human interaction" can profoundly influence (harm) the heart. In this instance, he is talking about the physical organ that pumps blood throughout the body. The loss of love has great consequences. This is particularly true between children and parents, between husbands and wives.

We are all products of the culture in which we were reared. Being on a college campus for several years leaves a cultural imprint. Religious distinctives and national history are cultural influences. When people from different cultures are mixed together, relationship difficulties are bound to increase.

Some years ago my father-in-law was hospitalized for cancer. He wanted me to be with him, so I canceled some speaking engagements, and we spent his last weeks together. While I was at the hospital, I met a patient—a young housewife about the age of our daughters. My wife and I had known her parents. She had a fine Christian husband and children. She asked that I come and visit her, and the reason for her hospitalization soon became apparent.

She was under deep emotional distress. She felt that her father had rejected her and this was more than she could bear. Her parents were immigrants from a country where the demonstration of love and pain are frowned upon. It was my privilege to explain the impact that different cultures have upon communications and relationships. I spoke to her very firmly and said, "Your father does love you, and he loves you very much." With this clarification, the hurt in her soul began to heal.

SIN AND THE VIOLATION OF ONE'S CONSCIENCE: These together are a major cause of woundedness. Nearly 3,000 years ago, Solomon spoke of the conscience as "the candle of the LORD, searching all the inward parts of the belly" (Proverbs 20:27). Our conscience is a wonderful agent. It is not unusual to read of someone who had wisely confessed to a crime in response to his or her conscience. This important matter is dealt with in some detail in chapter three where we discuss "The Conscience and Guilt."

THE SIN OF POSSESSIVENESS: We handle our emotions much better if, in our mind, God's ownership is a settled fact.

How extensive is God's ownership of your dear wife or husband, your children, career, home, car, and money? If someone dents the fender of God's car, it is much easier to be calm than when someone damages a car that is a closely held possession. Christians who are walking with God as the Lord of their life need not take unkind remarks personally because God is really their owner and He will handle the problem in His own way. "Every word of God is pure: he is a shield unto them that put their trust in him" (Proverbs 30:5).

Wisdom dictates that we be prepared in advance for events such as the loss of a loved one. These losses test our peace of mind and endurance. Every promise from the Bible quoted in this book is based upon the fact that God, Who knows all and is all caring, is the owner of all things. God, as the owner, is comparable to the hub of a wheel. The hub with many spokes reaching to its center is the power for carrying heavy loads. We best respect God as the owner of all things because He is the center that enables us to experience heavy loads and be victorious. God, as the hub of our lives, minimizes the hurt and distortions that come from emotionally-charged events.

"What? know ye not that your body is the temple of the Holy Ghost which is in you, which ye have of God, and ye are not your own? For ye are bought with a price [not our works or knowledge, but Christ's gift]: therefore glorify God in your body, and in your spirit, which are God's" (I Corinthians 6:19-20).

Possessiveness also tends to destroy the enhancements associated with cooperation. Extraordinary success usually involves a team effort where the combined product or service will exceed what individuals working alone can accomplish. The emotions of possessiveness soon eliminate people from participation because success depends upon humility and sharing the credit with others. The success of the potentially most capable person I have ever known was undermined because of emotional immaturity.

Frederic Bastiat writing *The Law,* and Charles H. Spurgeon both lamented the possessiveness of people who believe they must rule over others. Bastiat addressed the concern that laws should be written in a way that would curtail supremacists and preserve responsible liberty at the same time. Spurgeon deplored pastors and missionaries who from a distance seek to impose their will for operational decisions upon other pastors and missionaries instead of allowing them the freedom to make these decisions locally. Hierarchical micromanagement destroys incentive and progress.

Sound thinking and peace of mind are a matter of trusting God. We will have disappointments, but walking in the shadow of His grace leads to victory. "Rest in the LORD, and wait patiently for him [God]: fret not thyself because of him [who does evil] who prospereth in his way [appears to prosper], because of the man who bringeth wicked devices to pass [that will come to naught]" (Psalm 37:7).

Chapter Ten

Helping the Wounded

**Blessed is the man that endureth temptation: for when
he is tried, he shall receive the crown of life, which the Lord
hath promised to them that love him. James 1:12**

What can we do for those who are suffering emotional pain?
First, of course, we need to address any of their needs for
medical attention. When people do not want help or have
suffered an irreplaceable loss, we must expect that healing
will take much time and prayer. Sometimes people view the
need for help as a sign of failure, and these people will not
expose themselves to those whom they do not trust.

Typically, there are at least five people involved in helping
the wounded.

The first person involved is the Lord, Who knows the root
cause for our emotional pain. We approach this problem
looking to God, not man. It is important that the wounded
person understand that God wants what is best for him and
that he is very important to the Lord and to us.

"For the word of God is quick, and powerful, and sharper than any twoedged sword, piercing even to the dividing asunder of soul and spirit, and of the joints and marrow, and is a discerner of the thoughts and intents of the heart. Neither is there any creature that is not manifest in his sight: but all things are naked and opened unto the eyes of him with whom we have to do. Seeing then that we have a great high priest, that is passed into the heavens, Jesus the Son of God, let us hold fast our profession. For we have not an high priest which cannot be touched with the feeling of our infirmities; but was in all points tempted like as we are, yet without sin. Let us therefore come boldly unto the throne of grace, that we may obtain mercy, and find grace to help in time of need" (Hebrews 4:12-16).

The second person involved is the wounded person. This person's emotions may be holding him back from accepting God's help. The hurt in his mind is not imaginary. If the problem stems from betrayal by a loved one, the hurt may be very deep. The sight or even the thought of the one who caused the woundedness may nauseate him and make him physically ill. The wounded can have no peace if he does not let God intervene on his behalf (see Dr. Franklin's experience, page 70).

Third, I, the writer of this book, come with experience, but there is much more that is unknown than is known by me on the subject. It is quite likely, however, that God's answer to a friend's emotional problem is tucked away in the Bible verses in this book.

The fourth person involved is you, because you care. "Beyond prayer," you ask, "what shall I do to help my friend? Have I already been too involved? If not in me, in whom is the wounded person more likely to trust and confide? How shall I involve that person?" Have the helper persons whose thoughts are under the Spirit's control sought to bring reconciliation between those involved? Our God who raised Christ from the dead wants to see your friend restored!

Finally, there are others of influence within the circle of concern who may be part of God's plan for helping the person recover. However, it is important that we protect confidentiality. And in embarrassing matters, only those who are directly part of the situation should be inside the loop. A loving attitude and ongoing prayer are priorities for those who know the wounded person's need.

Counseling should be screened through three keys to peace of mind. Painting a word picture of these principles and their spiritual significance may help the wounded person.

First, what is it that has caused the woundedness? No two problems are exactly the same. The ministry of the counselor in this regard is to listen with concern and care, to thoughtfully inquire, and to offer helpful suggestions.

In cases where the woundedness was caused by another person (whom we will tentatively call the assailant), has the wounded one confronted the other person and sought reconciliation? Is the alleged assailant listening and taking the concerns of the wounded person seriously? If not, would he be willing to talk this over with me as a third party?

When a person reads God's Word on relevant matters and earnestly prays, we can expect that the individual will improve. If, however, he is unwilling to turn to God, then he is looking for help in the wrong direction.

Second, the presence of emotions should be factored into the search for healing. It is important for the counselor to understand that emotions have a way of getting the rational mind to subordinate itself to harmful emotions and justify that which is, in fact, wrong. Also, the emotions of self-pity, hopelessness, and anger work in opposition to God's healing. As Satan, the father of these lies and bitterness, well knows, such emotions stand in opposition to and render one inaccessible to God.

We aid the wounded by helping them gain control of their thoughts. In the previous chapter, we reviewed eight behavioral patterns that contribute to woundedness. In every case, yielding to emotions rather than to God and rational evaluation may have been a key factor. The nature of problems comes into view when untamed emotions cause one or more of the people involved to take action based on wrong assessments.

Satan wants the mind of the wounded person to be imprisoned by resentment and defeat. These emotions should be set aside. We belong to God; offenses are first and foremost against Him, not us! Every Christian is a recipient of God's grace. We cannot appropriate God's power for healing while at the same time denying this grace (harboring resentment) toward an offender. At first, however, it may not be possible for the wounded party to abandon misleading emotions and turn the hurt over to God. Even if their complaints are unjustified, they need to be received respectfully!

Promote optimism and hope by encouraging the hurting person to focus upon the half of the glass that is full rather than the empty half. At a restaurant some distance from our community, I noticed a man my wife and I had known for many years. I approached him and his wife at their table for a brief visit. Both had lost a spouse prior to their marriage to each other.

It was apparent that the lady was sad that day. My wife and I and the husband had been friends of a young man named Jim Williams. Jim was in his late teens, bed-ridden, and totally paralyzed from the neck down. Nevertheless, he was perhaps the happiest person we have ever known. Jim exuded the radiant testimony of a joyful person. This positive transformation from such a horrific situation has as its basis our relationship and position with God. "Now the Lord is that Spirit: and where the Spirit of the Lord is, there is liberty. But we all, with open face beholding as in a glass the glory of the Lord, are changed into the same image from glory to glory, even as by the Spirit of the Lord" (II Corinthians 3:17-18).

As I was chatting with the couple, I told the lady about Jim Williams, and encouraged her to look upon the half of the glass that is full. We do not normally expect an immediate response in situations like this but her countenance changed. As I left, she thanked me. "Who comforteth us in all our tribulation, that we may be able to comfort them which are in any trouble, by the comfort wherewith we ourselves are comforted of God" (II Corinthians 1:4).

Third, a prerequisite to healing is that the wounded one repent for assuming that he can solve his own problem. We simply are not equipped to carry and handle such heavy burdens on our own. God's ways are not our ways. He wants to carry the load. Without His help, wholeness and peace of mind in this sin-cursed world are not possible. Confessing and repenting of the sin of self-sufficiency are keys to healing. Repentance is changing one's mind. It may involve a prayer like the following: "God, this problem is Yours. Forgive me for interfering. I ask You to handle this problem as you see best!" It is our old nature that causes the woundedness to be so severe in the first place.

John the Baptist said of Christ, "He must increase, but I must decrease." What we want is God's will, and it is His will that we be healed. "I am crucified with Christ: nevertheless I live; yet not I, but Christ liveth in me: and the life which I now live in the flesh I live by the faith of the Son of God, who loved me, and gave himself for me" (Galatians 2:20).

"The LORD is nigh unto them that are of a broken heart; and saveth such as be of a contrite spirit" (Psalm 34:18). Healing cannot happen until we come to God in prayer and reject the sin of self-will and any other sin. Taking responsibility for our sin is key. The counselor's goal is to help the person bring the cause for woundedness to the surface of his mind and then give the burden over to God. "If we confess our sins, he is faithful and just to forgive us our sins, and to cleanse us from all unrighteousness" (I John 1:9). It is not by works that we are justified (sin is paid for already) but by faith in the finished work of Christ. When confession and repentance occur, God's grace can come in and heal.

The causes for woundedness are often offenses imposed upon us by others. God does not intend that we carry the burden of these offenses. Woundedness is a spiritual matter. The offense is first and foremost a sin against God our Father, not against us! We are His children. When we take such an offense personally, we must repent and give it over to God's care.

Sometimes woundedness is a direct result of our own sin. Counselors can help the wounded person by confronting the cause for woundedness, whatever it may be. Satan wins if we pretend there is no sin to confront. We win and carry far less of a burden when we take responsibility for our attitude and actions.

A wounded person may pray a prayer like this: "I confess, I did _____, and that was wrong. Forgive me for my sin. Lord, forgive me for trying to solve this problem by hiding it. Forgive me for interfering with Your healing work in my life."

> The transaction between God and self often takes time because we tend to be mentally and spiritually slow in coming to Him. It may be well to review the lists of causes for woundedness (chapter nine), the hindrances to effective prayer (chapter five), and how to listen to God (chapter six). When we pray over these matters, we are talking to our memory bank as well as to God. This is the process of accepting God's provision that comes through our union with Christ.

The work of the Spirit of Christ in the heart of hurting individuals is of great importance. Romans 8:26 is a wonderful provision of God that may help in the healing process, a key to restoring peace and the blessing of God's power in one's life.

"Likewise the Spirit also helpeth our infirmities: for we know not what we should pray for as we ought: but the Spirit itself maketh intercession for us with groanings which cannot be uttered" (Romans 8:26). Our prayer for healing emotional pain need not be complicated: "Lord, I am anxious to identify, confess and forsake the sins in my past that have been overlooked. Please help me see the Infirmities' that I know not. Bring any sin that is hindering my relationship with You to my attention so that I can confess it and receive Your forgiveness." **A sincere prayer such as this has brought blessing and release to many.**

When we confess our sin and place the burden on God's shoulder, He can then work through us to remove the woundedness. It is by the power of His grace we are able to reach out in love toward the offender and pray for his or her well-being.

F. N. Peloube once said: "Wounds once healed [do] leave a scar behind them. It is harder to forgive ourselves than to forgive others. But sin, when once wholly forgiven, should be accepted as forgiven, and we should have such trust in Christ who forgives that we shall not waste our strength and joy in vain and bitter regrets. Let the dead past bury its dead.' There is a divinity that shapes our ends, rough-hew them how He will. This is the joy of perfect faith in the divine providence: that God overrules all men and all events and will compel all to aid in carrying out the purposes of his love. This is the final stage of penitence. The knowledge that God has prevented our sin from doing the [further] harm makes needless the bitterness and despair with which we view forgiven sin in our past. At the same time it strengthens the most effectual bulwark in our mind for rejecting sin—obedience to the holy and over-ruling God."

Without experiencing setbacks we would not know the power of God. "Shew me thy ways, O LORD; teach me thy paths" (Psalm 25:4). "And he said unto me, My grace is sufficient for thee: for my strength is made perfect in weakness. Most gladly therefore will I rather glory in my infirmities [difficulties that will cause me to rely upon God], that the power of Christ may rest upon me" (II Corinthians 12:9). "Humble yourselves therefore under the mighty hand of God, that he may exalt you in due time" (I Peter 5:6).

Choices: When we have an unforgiving spirit or are laden with other sin we have two choices. We can repent and accept God's provision for peace of mind purchased by Christ's sacrifice on the Cross, or continue to reject the love and care of God's grace.

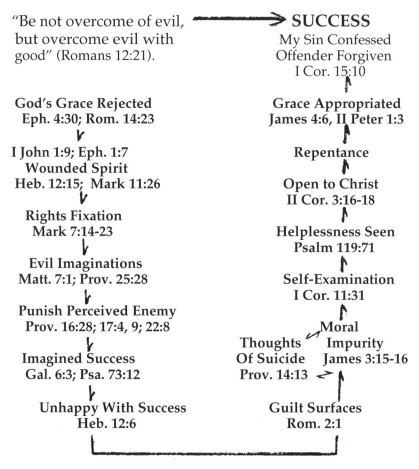

"Be not overcome of evil, ———————➤ SUCCESS
but overcome evil with   My Sin Confessed
good" (Romans 12:21).   Offender Forgiven
                                    I Cor. 15:10
                                         ▲

God's Grace Rejected   Grace Appropriated
Eph. 4:30; Rom. 14:23   James 4:6, II Peter 1:3
        ▼   ▲
I John 1:9; Eph. 1:7   Repentance
  Wounded Spirit   ▲
Heb. 12:15; Mark 11:26   Open to Christ
        ▼   II Cor. 3:16-18
  Rights Fixation   ▲
  Mark 7:14-23   Helplessness Seen
        ▼   Psalm 119:71
  Evil Imaginations   ▲
Matt. 7:1; Prov. 25:28   Self-Examination
        ▼   I Cor. 11:31
Punish Perceived Enemy   ▲
Prov. 16:28; 17:4, 9; 22:8   Moral
        ▼   Thoughts ⟋ Impurity
  Imagined Success   Of Suicide   James 3:15-16
  Gal. 6:3; Psa. 73:12 Prov. 14:13 ⟵ ▲
        ▼   │
Unhappy With Success   Guilt Surfaces
   Heb. 12:6   Rom. 2:1
        └_____┘

"And through [the emotion of]
covetousness . . . they with feigned
words make merchandise of you" (II Peter 2:3a).

As long as grace is operative, man's failure is never final.
"Charity never faileth" (I Corinthians 13:8a).

When humility and an appreciation for God prevail in our heart, God replaces our woundedness with peace. John Bunyan was a person like you and me. He felt the anguish of wrongful imprisonment that lasted for twelve years! John Bunyan said, "It is hard to get down in the valley of humility. The descent is steep and rugged, but it is very fruitful, fertile, and beautiful when we once get there."

We are branches created in God's image, and He is the vine. To defy creation and allow ourselves to become rooted in the world rather than in God generates havoc. Rejecting the temptation to sin calls for singleness of mind. The Bible says we are to submit ourselves to God! This involves moving ourselves away from worldly situations because, given the opportunity, our old nature will betray us. "Draw nigh to God, and he will draw nigh to you. Cleanse your hands, ye sinners; and purify your hearts, ye double minded" (James 4:8).

"And let us [as believers] consider one another to provoke unto love and to good works: Not forsaking the assembling of ourselves together, as the manner of some is; but exhorting one another" (Hebrews 10:24-25).

The following is a list of questions that God may use to give answers and direction.

1. Do I have all the facts surrounding the problem?

2. Who and what precipitated the woundedness?
Whether or not the one who caused the woundedness is guilty of wrongdoing is irrelevant to the wounded person. He needs to identify the event before he can turn it over to God. "But he that lacketh these things is blind, and cannot see afar off, and hath forgotten that he was purged from his old sins" (II Peter 1:9).

3. Could the woundedness have been caused by gossip?
Defiling gossip usually comes from the lips of a trusted person. Maybe this person now sees the damage that has been done. This person may be the one who could help the wounded to be restored and to regain peace of mind.

4. If the wounded person is rejecting help, why is he?
What change in the environment or context for counseling
   might induce a willingness to open up?
Would he respond to a person who, with God's help, has
   already conquered the same problem?
Does the problem reflect a cultural difference that needs an
   explanation?
Is there a need for the renewed power of God's love? Are
   we, as God's helpers, demonstrating God's love?
Would sharing weaknesses of my own help him to
   appreciate help and be willing to identify and expose his
   problem?
Would asking him the favor of helping in a project that is
   beneficial to others cause him to open up and share his
   own hurts?

**5. Would he pursue new activities helpful to the mind and
body?** Young physicians are subject to the military draft in
times such as the Vietnam conflict. Some, I am told, think
that is not so bad but then become angry when they lose
control of their lives because of military duty. Wisely, as a
diversion from the obsession of anger, some will turn their
attention to self-improvement, working at such things as
lowering their golf score.

6. Would the gift of an appropriate book help?

**7. Would painting a word picture of a similar situation that
had been successfully resolved be of help?**

**8. Am I, as a friend and helper or counselor, giving
adequate prayer to the matter?**

**9. Has the person been under the burden so long that he
sees the situation as hopeless?** The person may be restored
to hopefulness by comforting Scripture, a listening ear, and
genuine sympathy.

**10. Is he operating in a goals vacuum and perceiving goals
as hopeless?** Re-establishing goals might cause him to accept

help and share his troubles. Ask the following questions:

Is what you are now doing moving you toward your goals for life?

What do you see as your primary life goals? If you could make a significant change, what would it be?

As a worker, as a husband, as a _____, what do you do best?

Review with him the reasons for setting the defeated self aside, turning to God, and pursuing a captivating, God-honoring goal. (Refer to the section in chapter three entitled "God's Grace, Decision-Making, and Emotions").

1. Is he grieving?
Is he tearful? Tears can be helpful. Recovery from irreplaceable losses means adapting to a different context for daily activity.

God can give him a new life that is meaningful. In a limited way, problems from a loss and the grief that follows resemble the problems faced by those who have been bedridden and unconscious for several months. These people may have to learn to talk and walk all over again.

2. Could any of the following ideas be the basis for encouragement and a breakthrough? Ask . . .
Do you look back with fondness to the time you accepted Christ?

What do you like to do for recreation?

What else do you really like to do?

What would add to your feeling of peace and safety?

What people or things are hindering you from reaching your goals?

3. Is he in a Bible study program?
When our mind is continuously bolstered by Scripture, our perspective, judgment, and goals improve significantly. See Hebrews 4:12-16 (quoted earlier in this chapter).

4. Is his perception of the circumstances unbiblical? It is helpful to hurting persons if they understand that problems which come our way have the benefit of establishing our faith and building our character. Self-analysis which penetrates darkened understanding has as its basis a thankful spirit and genuine trust in God. Consequently, people who are hurting need to be reminded that a conscious choice to trust God is the basis for the understanding essential for solving problems. **This means they need to humbly bring every thought into obedience and subjection to His Word for His help.** Our thoughts can then be shaped and prioritized according to the truth (God's Word). It is this type of relationship with the all-knowing and all-powerful God that makes us into successful overcomers. "But we had the sentence of death [insoluble problem] in ourselves, that we should not trust in ourselves, but in God which raiseth the dead: Who delivered us from so great a death, and doth deliver: in whom we trust that he will yet deliver us" (II Corinthians 1:9-10). "For I know the thoughts that I think toward you, saith the LORD, thoughts of peace, and not of evil, to give you an expected end. Then shall ye call upon me, and ye shall go and pray unto me, and I will hearken unto you" (Jeremiah 29:11-12).

Questions for the hurting person to ask:

1. To my knowledge, what relationships are causing me to experience conflict or to be discontent, bitter, hurt, or angry?

2. How would you, as a counselor, suggest that I proceed to improve the situation?

3. Who are the people and offenses that have disrupted my peace of mind?
   Person's name_____
   The offense is_____
   Person's name_____
   The offense is_____

4. What authority persons do I resent?
   Person's name_____
   The offense is_____
   Person's name_____
   The offense is_____

5. Who are the people for whom I sacrifice yet who do not respond as they should?
   Person's name_____
   The offense is_____
   Person's name_____
   The offense is_____

Agreement with God and His Word are essential!

6. Have I personally invited Christ into my life to be my Lord and Savior from sin (John 3:16)?   Yes ❑ No ❑

7. Do I recognize that, though being saved is essential, salvation does not empower me to go my own way and then expect God to give me victory (Proverbs 3)?
   Yes ❑ No ❑

8. Do I believe that God knows my need and will guide my thinking if I place my total trust in Him?   Yes ❑ No ❑

9. Do I accept the fact that I was created to be under authority and that the solution to my problem lies with acceptance of God's instruction?   Yes ❑ No ❑

10. Do I understand that God's timing may not be what I prefer and that working with Him is a character-building process?   Yes ❑ No ❑

11. Do I understand that the world, Satan, and the wicked nature within are the enemies?   Yes ❑ No ❑

12. Do I agree that I have made mistakes which have hurt others and myself?   Yes ❑ No ❑

13. Is my attitude toward problems wrong? Remember that chief among the ways that Satan confuses our thinking and prevents the healing of our soul is the deceptive lure of sin-laden habits. Given half an opportunity, Satan uses imaginations and unrighteous emotions along with the flesh. "But he giveth more grace. Wherefore he saith, God resisteth the proud, but giveth grace unto the humble" (James 4:6). "Create in me a clean heart, O God; and renew a right spirit within me. Cast me not away from thy presence; and take not thy holy spirit from me. Restore unto me the joy of thy salvation; and uphold me with thy free spirit" (Psalm 51:10-12).

Yes ❑ No ❑

14. Have I have sought to root out any ungratefulness toward God? "In every thing [including testings] give thanks: for this is the will of God in Christ Jesus concerning you" (I Thessalonians 5:18). "And we know that all things work together for good to them that love God, to them who are the called according to his purpose" (Romans 8:28). Yes ❑ No ❑

15. Do I accept the fact that the other person who is a part of this problem is just as important to You, dear Lord, as I am important to You? Yes ❑ No ❑

16. Do I recognize the importance of continual prayer for truth and grace toward others? "And when ye stand praying, forgive, if ye have ought against any: that your Father also which is in heaven may forgive you your trespasses. But if ye do not forgive, neither will your Father which is in heaven forgive your trespasses" (Mark 11:25-26). Yes ❑ No ❑

17. Lord, do I believe that no matter what other people do, You can give me the ability to see through the problem and to trust You enough to have peace? Yes ❑ No ❑

18. Do I realize that I cannot expect God to help me if I tell Him how He is to solve the problem? Am I willing to change when I learn from God's Word where I have been wrong? Yes ❑ No ❑

19. Do I understand that I injure my own soul and unleash harmful emotions when I refuse to forgive offenders, and that others need and deserve (because of the Cross) my forgiving grace just as I need and deserve (because of the Cross) the forgiving grace of others?   Yes ❏ No ❏

20. Do I place the offender's evil against me upon God's shoulders and truly forgive the offender?   Yes ❏ No ❏

21. Do I know that Christ has taken the burden from me because I can now pray for the welfare of the offender and see him without feeling the need to punish him?
                                                   Yes ❏ No ❏

"Judge not [Christ says], and ye shall not be judged [lose God's blessing]: condemn not, and ye shall not be condemned: forgive, and ye shall be forgiven: Give, and it shall be given unto you; good measure, pressed down, and shaken together, and running over, shall men give into your bosom. For with the same measure that ye mete withal it shall be measured to you again" (Luke 6:37-38).

It is God Who gives faithful believers a mind for rising above adversity. Only our rejection of His enabling power (grace beyond human ability) can hinder peace and the capacity to live according to I Corinthians 13 and Galatians 5:22-26.

In situations where restoration, which is the first priority, fails and the dynamic of an organization is endangered, God's Matthew 18:15-18 sequence may be appropriate. "Moreover if thy brother shall trespass against thee, go and tell him his fault between thee and him alone: if he shall hear thee, thou hast gained thy brother. But if he will not hear thee, then take with thee one or two more [impartial people], that in the mouth of two or three witnesses every word [its legitimacy and seriousness] may be established. And if he shall neglect to hear them, tell it unto the church [people affected]: but if he neglect to hear the church [members' assessment of the offense], let him be unto thee as a heathen man and a publican [separate from him and pray for him].

Verily I say unto you, Whatsoever ye shall bind on earth shall be bound in heaven: and whatsoever ye shall loose on earth shall be loosed in heaven."

> **Enduring relationships involve humility, transparency, collaboration, and shared goals.**

The Presbyterian Alexander Whyte (1836-1921) aptly expressed the spiritual role of humility: "Do you not know what it is in you, and about you, that lands you in such nakedness and pain? You know quite well. Fight every day against no one else but yourself; and against nothing else but every secret emotion of pride, and anger, and malice, and love of evil. Every blow you deal to these deadly things of which your heart is full is another safe and sure step back to God. At every such stroke . . . at your own sin God will by all that come back to you; till, at last, He will fill your whole soul with Himself. That was the way, and it was in no other way, that Enoch 'walked with God.' And you too will walk with God, and God with you, just in the measure in which you put on humility, and put off pride; and fill your heart full of the meekness and lowly-mindedness of the Son of God [humiliated beyond measure, Christ Who had no sin, gave His life on the cross in payment for our sins]. To hold your peace when you are reproved, that is a sure step toward God. To let a slight, a contempt, an affront, an insult, a scoff, a sneer, fall on your head like an excellent oil, and on your heart like your true dessert—'with that man will I dwell,' says the God of Israel and the God and Father of our Lord Jesus Christ." (From the book of sermons, *Lord, Teach Us to Pray*, London: Hodder and Stoughton, March, 1922.)

Our role as a helper is to be caring but factual and non-emotional participants. We must never give up! We help by encouraging those who are hurting to graft God's ways into their attitude.

"I beseech you therefore, brethren, by the mercies of God, that ye present your bodies a living sacrifice, holy, acceptable unto God, which is your reasonable service [it is a bargain]. And be not conformed to this world: but be ye transformed by the renewing of your mind [know and accept God's Word], that ye may prove what is that good, and acceptable, and perfect, will of God" (Romans 12:1-2).

In the next two chapters we will shift from concerns for those who are wounded in mind and spirit to the practical procedures involved in overcoming everyday barriers to success.

Chapter Eleven

Joseph,* God's Pattern for an Overcomer

Then Joseph could not refrain himself before all them that stood by him; and he cried, Have every man to go out from me. And there stood no man with him, while Joseph made himself known unto his brethren. And he wept aloud: and the Egyptians and the house of Pharaoh heard. And Joseph said unto his brethren, Come near to me, I pray you. And they came near. And he said, I am Joseph your brother, whom ye sold into Egypt. Now therefore be not grieved, nor angry with yourselves, that ye sold me hither: for God did send me before you to preserve life. Genesis 45:1-2, 4-5

Joseph knew the pain of mental and spiritual woundedness. As in the life of Job, the scene here is opened for us to see the divine purpose in Joseph's afflictions. Joseph's difficulties were hidden as they occurred. As in our lives, God's purposes eventually became apparent.

---

* *"The Life of Joseph,"* modified from a Sunday school lesson by F. N. Peloubet, D. D., 1894.

God's Purposes

1. The drastic change in Joseph's life was probably necessary. As a favorite son, he was in great danger of being spoiled. Then there were portions of his nature that would remain undeveloped except in circumstances away from home. Circumstances, prosperous or adverse, do not alter character, but they are the means of developing character.

2. God used all these things in carrying out His plans. He had a great work for Joseph to do. He knew that the Israelites needed, first of all, the long discipline of residence in Egypt to fit them to become the people of God. Second, by contact with a highly civilized people they received an education in arts, law and government, —unlikely prospects in Canaan. Third, in Egypt they would not adulterate their race and lose their distinctiveness through intermarriage with the Canaanites. Finally, their marvelous redemption would teach them to have faith in God and His omniscient care.

Good Out of Evil

It is a comfort to know that God rules over all and that He can use the evil which men do in such a way as to defeat their plans and bring forth good.

Practical Observations

1. Selfishness is the rich soil in which all wrong passions flourish.

2. Envy is diabolical. Other sins yield some short-term pleasure, but envy offers nothing but torment. It is the soil of selfishness in which crimes flourish.

3. A saint in his worst of trials has greater happiness than a sinner in his best triumph.

4. The crime that results from envy brings with it a long train of sorrows to many persons.

5. God brought good out of this evil, but it was evil in itself and would have brought only evil had not God intervened.

6. Jacob deceived his father, and his children deceived him. As the saying goes, "Curses, like chickens, come home to roost."

7. Sins are social; crime begets crime. Envy, hatred, murder, lying, and unkindness to parents were all united together in this transaction.

8. Here is inspiration and comfort for our disappointing hours. Joseph, in the pit or as a slave, could see no way in which his captivity could work out for good, **yet he was faithful**.

9. The mills of God grind slowly, but "Be sure your sin will find you out" (Numbers 32:23).

Joseph, Ruler in Egypt—Genesis 41:38-48
Golden Text—*Them that honor Me I will honor* (I Samuel 2:30).
   The Section of History—Genesis 39-41
   New Testament Light—(1) The story (Acts 7:9-11); (2) Peter in prison (Acts 12:4-11); (3) God's providence (Romans 8:28); (4) faithful in few things, ruler over many (Matthew 25:21, 23; Luke 19:26); (5) promises of success (Matthew 6:33; Mark 10:29-30). Psalm 105:16-22 refers to God's wonderful and loving providence over His people at this time.
   Time—1716 B.C., thirteen years after Joseph was sold to the Midianites.
   Place—It is generally supposed that the capitol of Egypt at this time was Zoan, near one of the mouths of the Nile River.
   Joseph was now 30 years old (41:46). He was 17 when he was sold into Egypt (37:2). It is supposed that he spent 10 of the 13 intervening years as a slave of Potiphar and 3 in the king's prison.
   Jacob, now 121 years old, was still living at Hebron.

Explanatory
I. Thirteen Years of Preparation—Joseph in "The Testings" of Life.
   Ten Years of Service and Trial. Joseph, when he reached Egypt, was sold to Potiphar, "the captain of the guard." The military class in Egypt ranked next to the priesthood, and the entire force consisted of 410,000 men who were divided into two corps, one thousand serving as the king's body-guards. Potiphar was probably the captain of one of these, and was consequently a man of great honor and influence.

Three Years in Prison. At the end of ten years, another bitter trial came to Joseph. After long resisting temptation, his very goodness was made the occasion of an unjust accusation. Without trial he was cast into prison. In Genesis 41:14, it is called "the dungeon." In Psalms 105:17, 18, we are told that his feet were hurt with fetters; he was laid in iron. The imprisonment was at first severe. But God kept him and afterwards gave him a better life of waiting upon the other prisoners.

Steps in Joseph's Training and Preparation. (1) His troubles were severe. (2) He learned trust in God. He simply clung closer to God, as should we. (3) He had long opportunity to study himself and his needs. (4) Whatever the circumstances, Joseph did what was right. He not only *looked* on the bright side, he *worked* on the bright side. The way to be ready for larger fields is to be faithful in the smaller ones. It is good to remember that the particular sphere we are in is of very small importance compared with what we do in that sphere. Humility is just as beautiful in a hovel as in a palace. Truth, courage, and honor are no more noble on a throne than in a factory or on a farm. Love, gentleness, and self-denial are as blessed in the kitchen as in the parlor, or in the prison as in the court. (5) The injustice done to him did not make him unjust to others. (6) He was observant and diligent in the development of his mind. (7) The work he had to do for Potiphar was excellent training for the future. Egyptian courtiers were often rich. One, for example, had 835 oxen, 220 cows and calves, 760 asses, 2,235 goat-like sheep, and 974 goats. For Joseph to care for all these would require much learning, preparation and executive ability.

II. Links in the Chain of Divine Providence by Which Joseph Was Delivered.

The story of the dreams of the butler and baker and Joseph's aid to them is given in Genesis, chapter 40. Joseph continued in prison for two years after showing kindness to the released cupbearer, who ungratefully forgot all about Joseph. Then, when God sent two strange dreams to Pharaoh, the butler remembered Joseph. He was called out of prison and, receiving the interpretation from God, told Pharaoh that the two dreams had the same meaning. In this New Testament dispensation dreams are no longer needed or used by God, but in the Old Testament God often used dreams to warn of coming events. Seven years of abundance were to be followed by seven years of extraordinary dearth. Joseph counseled Pharaoh to appoint a qualified person to have authority over all the land, that he might store up the surplus corn of the seven years of plenty for the seven years of famine.

There are Two Elements in every life—the **Divine** and the **Human**—God's providence and man's free choice. Our success in life depends upon both. All the open doors in the world are of no use if we have not prepared to enter them. What are opportunities for business to one who has not learned business? What are libraries to one who refuses to learn to read? We have seen the human element in Joseph's life in his faithfulness and discipline.

The Divine Element interrelates with the human element. All through his life there were circumstances beyond his control. This divine element opened doors. It prepared ways, it directed the concurring actions of men, and Joseph experienced enhanced character development.

III. Joseph Exalted to Be Governor of Egypt—Verses 38-45.

38. *And Pharaoh said*, in response to the advice Joseph had given, *Can we find such a one as this is*, for the carrying out of the proposed plans? Doubtless the story of Joseph during his slavery and his prison life was familiar to them, and by his past actions, as well as his present wisdom, they saw clearly that he was especially fitted for the proposed work. *A man in whom the Spirit of God is.* He attributed Joseph's wisdom and fidelity to the true source. One in whom God's Spirit dwells (1) will have wisdom and unfailing common sense; (2) will be faithful to all his duties; (3) will have his commitment to overcoming obstacles attended by God's blessing.

39. *Forasmuch as God hath shewed thee all this.* We see in Joseph a striking illustration of the truth of the promise, "Them that honor Me, I will honor." If God had shown Joseph much, He would also give him wisdom in the future.

Such a man would be invaluable as a ruler. *There is none so discreet*, refers to Joseph's intelligence, and clear insight into matters and his comprehension of their true character, while *wise* denotes a capacity of devising measures to gain desired ends.

40. *Thou shalt be over my house,* my palace, including all the officers and ministers of the kingdom.

42. *And Pharaoh took off his ring.* The ring was undoubtedly a signet, or seal-ring, which gave validity to the documents to which it was affixed and by the delivery of which, therefore, Pharaoh delegated to Joseph the chief authority in the state.

43. *Made him to ride in the second chariot.* Thus arrayed, Joseph was placed in Pharaoh's second chariot (next to Pharaoh's) and they led a splendid procession through the city.

44. *I am Pharaoh.* That is, I, by my authority as the Emperor, raise Joseph to this position. *And without thee shall no man lift up his hand or foot in all the land of Egypt.* Joseph's authority was to be absolute and universal.

IV. Joseph's Great Work—Verses 46, 48.

46. *And Joseph went out from the presence of Pharaoh.* He did not remain among the pleasures of the court but immediately went to his new duties. *And went throughout all the land of Egypt* to issue the proper orders and, in order to see their execution, made an immediate survey to determine the sight and size of the storehouses required for the different quarters of the country.

48. *And he gathered up all the food of the seven years.* According to his own advice to Pharaoh, Joseph gathered up a fifth part (v. 34). This was the government tax. Doubtless the people also stored up grain for themselves, but according to their faith which was much less than Joseph's. This tax continued during the seven years of plenty.

True Success. His success consisted (1) in his worthy character and fitness to serve God and man, (2) in his work in helping a great number of people, (3) in his proclamation of God to an idolatrous people, and (4) in the blessings he brought upon his father's family.

Lessons from Joseph in Egypt

1. There is a divine and human element in every successful life.

2. The trials and experiences are meant to prepare us for greater success.

3. So our whole life is a school for the future life. "We know not what we shall be." We do not know what glorious work or place is before us.

4. But we do know that faithfulness in little things is the preparation for greater things. We work for God doing our best every day.

5. We cannot control our circumstances, but we can control what we shall do in the circumstances.

6. God's plans and promises never fail, though He may be long in working them out.

7. The abiding presence of God by His Holy Spirit, leading to obedience and pure motives, is the way to wisdom and to success. He that serves God with supreme devotion will serve man most faithfully.

8. There is always a demand for people who do their best.

9. Influence in the long run belongs to those who rid their minds of selfish aims. People feel themselves safe when with those who are unselfish.

10. Success is honoring God by doing what you can do well, and doing well whatever you can do.

11. There will always come a famine of sorts, but Christ has plenty to spare for all who will come to Him.

Subject: The Way to a Successful Life

Follow the story. **Apply** it to our present life. What did God do, and what was Joseph learning? He was learning about Egypt and obtaining an inside view of the people's characters and feelings, which no king on the throne could obtain. He was growing strong and self-reliant. He was learning kindness and the power of serving. He learned of the faithfulness of God and the importance of honoring God's ways rather than what seemed expedient. The difficulties would have been of no use to him if he had not learned to overcome them as they came along.

Illustration—John Bunyan could not understand why God should allow him to be imprisoned and shut out from his work for twelve precious years. He longed to preach the Gospel to the thousands of people waiting to hear him. He could not then see that by writing *Pilgrim's Progress* while he was in prison he would preach to millions instead of thousands, and for centuries instead of years.

Joseph Forgiving His Brethren—Genesis 45:1-15
Golden Text—*If thy brother trespass against thee, rebuke him; and if he repent, forgive him* [forgiveness is assumed; a better translation would be: "consider him restored"] (Luke 17:3).

The Section of History—Genesis 41:53-45:28
New Testament Light—(1) overcoming evil with good (Romans 12:20, 21); (2) how to treat enemies (Matthew 5:44; Romans 12:14); (3) forgiving (Matthew 6:12, 14-15; 18:21-35); (4) how God leads to repentance (Romans 2:4; Matthew 5:45).
Time—1707 B.C., the second year of the famine, 9 years after the last lesson and 22 after the sale of Joseph by his brothers.
Place—Heliopolis, in Egypt; situated on the Nile, near the mouth of the Nile. It was about 250 miles from Hebron, Jacob's home.
Jacob—About 130 years old. He is still living at Hebron with eleven of his sons.
Joseph—39 years old, of which he has spent 22 in Egypt, 13 of them as a slave and 9 as a governor. He has a wife and two children. Benjamin must be 24 or 25 years old.

I. A Panorama
The story that follows is a series of events from life. Each has its own way of instruction for us.
1. The Famine in Hebron. Jacob's family of 11 sons and many servants was on the brink of starvation.
2. The Caravan to Egypt. Ten brothers went to Egypt, leaving Benjamin at home. There were probably many beasts of burden besides those which the brothers rode. There would also have been servants.

3. Joseph's Rough Treatment of His Brothers. He denounced them as spies and imprisoned them partly in order to learn about his father without disclosing himself.

4. The Ghost of the Past. In their trouble, his brothers remembered what they had done to Joseph. The past confronted them. Reuben recounted how he had tried to save Joseph. Joseph himself overheard and understood all this, although they thought they were talking in a tongue unknown to him. Reuben's character and past actions were thus revealed to Joseph, and Joseph knew how to treat him.

5. Simeon, whom his father called self-willed, cruel, and fierce in anger (Genesis 49:5-7), was kept in prison as the one who most needed discipline, as doubtless the fiercest toward Joseph. The others were released after three days and returned home with provisions.

6. The Second Caravan. They could not go back to Egypt without Benjamin. The father refused to send Benjamin; starvation was at hand. Jacob finally consented with sad reluctance, and Benjamin went along. They took for the Egyptian governor a gift of spices which the famine had not destroyed.

7. The Second Reception. The touching scene at a feast: Joseph saw his own brother once more. Benjamin was given a portion. Joseph had to express his feelings in some way.

8. The Silver Cup was put in Benjamin's sack so he would be brought back, and no distinction would be made between the brothers who had sold Joseph. They returned to the capitol.

9. Judah's Noble and Touching Plea revealed his character to Joseph. This was Judah, who all "shall praise," the "lion's whelp," whose "sceptre shall not depart" (Genesis 49:8-10). In Judah's intercession for Benjamin he demonstrated the feeling that accompanies meaningful prayer.

10. Why Did Not Joseph's Brethren Recognize Him? (1) They were grown up when he left them, but Joseph left them as a beardless boy of seventeen, and he was now a man of forty. (2) They were in the shepherd dress in which he knew them, while he was robed in the magnificence of royalty. (3) They spoke in his native tongue while he spoke Egyptian, and to them only through an interpreter. (4) They had no expectation of seeing him in that position, but he knew the country from which they came.

11. Joseph's Treatment of His Brothers at first seems to be strange, but the reasons seemed to unfold as follows: (1) To learn all about them and their circumstances, so as to know what course to take. (2) To awaken their memories of the past and stimulate their conscience toward repentance. (3) To later render his forgiveness of the past more complete since they would know that it was in full view of all they had done. (4) To test his brothers and to see how worthy they were of the benefits that he could confer. He learned how they now treated their father, how they loved Benjamin, how kindly their feelings were toward one another. Their trials had greatly improved their character. (5) To show them that God had fulfilled his early dreams (Genesis 42:9); His interpretation of Pharaoh's dreams was therefore also correct, and God had been with him in life.

II. Joseph Reveals Himself—Verses 1-4.

When Joseph had sufficiently tested his brothers and found them tender of heart, full of kindness to Benjamin and his father, then Joseph saw that the hour had come to reveal himself to his brothers.

1. *Then Joseph could not refrain himself* (i.e., keep himself from showing his emotions) before all them that stood by him (i.e., the Egyptian officials of his household); and he cried (issued an instruction), he caused every Egyptian to leave, for two reasons. (1) His role forbids the presence of others at this unrestrained outburst of emotion among the brothers. Besides, (2) the workings of conscience bringing up unavoidable recollections of past errors are not to be unveiled to the public.

2. *And he wept aloud.* These were tears of emotion—pity and joy more than sorrow. *The Egyptians and the house of Pharaoh heard* the sound of Joseph weeping. Orientals tend to withhold the expression of their feelings. The news about his brothers became known and the Pharaoh was *pleased*, Genesis 45:16.

3. *I am Joseph.* The natural voice, the native tongue, the long-remembered features would all at once strike the brothers with great apprehension. *Doth my father yet live?* This question shows where Joseph's thoughts were. *They were troubled at his presence.* The memory of all the wrong they had done to their brother came upon their souls like an avalanche. They would have sooner expected thunder and lightening than to see their injured brother on a throne in Egypt. They knew they were in Joseph's power. If he should treat them as they once had treated him, there would be no hope for them.

4. *And Joseph said . . . I am Joseph your brother, whom ye sold into Egypt.* It was impossible to evade allusion to their earlier wickedness, but, rather than being angry and upbraiding, Joseph revealed a humble spirit of love and tender care.

Gospel Applications (1) Jesus seeks us before we know Him. (2) Before Jesus can come into our lives, there must be an awakening of our conscience. We must see and feel our sin. Then (3) we need to repent in dust and ashes, and show by our attitude that we repudiate the old evil and desire to do the good deeds of the new man. (4) Jesus comes to us as our brother. He is not ashamed to call us brethren (Hebrews 2:11). All brotherly feelings are in Him toward us. (5) He bids us come to Him (Matthew 11:28-30) and be not afraid, though (6) we have rejected and neglected Him. (7) Jesus forgives all the past. (8) Jesus comes to us to supply our needs, to save us from the spiritual famine of worldliness. (9) This salvation is not for us alone, but for our friends, our families, and our children. We are to go forth as demonstrations of God's divine abundance and invite all to accept Christ.

III. God Brings Good Out of Man's Evil—Verses 5-8.

5. *Now therefore be not grieved.* Joseph here shows the nobleness of his character. Wounds healed do leave scars behind them, and sometimes the memories make it harder to forgive ourselves than to forgive others. But sin, when forgiven, should be considered forgiven! We should trust in the forgiveness of Christ who paid for our sin instead of wasting our strength and joy in vain and bitter regrets.

"Let the dead past bury its dead." *For God did send me before you to preserve life.* God used their evil to accomplish His purpose. There is a divinity that shapes our ends, rough-hew them how He will. This is the joy of perfect faith in the divine providence, that God overrules all men and all events and will compel all to aid in carrying out the purposes of His love. This is the final stage of penitence. The knowledge that God has prevented our sin from doing additional harm erases the bitterness and despair with which we view forgiven sin in our past. At the same time it strengthens the most effectual bulwark in our mind for rejecting sin—obedience to the holy and over-ruling God.

6. *God sent me before you.* This phrase shows that God was bringing good out of their evil.

7. *So now it was not you that sent me hither, but God.* Although the brothers were guilty, God accomplished His will through their deed. They were to blame, but this thought made it easier, now that they had repented, to forgive themselves.

Note. First, it is impossible for us to judge whether or not any event is a blessing or a misfortune by simply looking at the event itself because we do not know the whole. Second, there is a danger of using the fact that good can come from evil as an excuse to sin. We should clearly see that the evil and its consequences are ours to avoid, and the good is God's to accomplish. It would be inconceivably horrible for this world if God were not able to bring good out of man's evil.

IV. Joseph Sends for His Father to Come Into Egypt—Verses 9-15.

8. *Haste ye, and go up to my father,* for every moment's delay lengthened the sorrow and anxiety of the aged patriarch.

9. *Thou shalt dwell in the land of Goshen.* It probably was an unsettled district, but rich in pastures and belonged in a very loose way to Egypt.

10. *And thy household.* In verse 18 Joseph speaks of "their households," showing that each of the patriarchs now had his own body of dependents, in addition to the larger clan which belonged to Jacob.

11. *And, behold, your eyes see.* There is no doubt of my identity, and you can thus prove to our father, Jacob, that there is no danger in accepting this invitation.

12. *And ye shall tell my father of all my glory.* Why? Not out of pride, but (1) to make him sure that his promise could be carried out; (2) to comfort his father in the good fortune that had come to his long-lost son; (3) to make it easier for the ten sons to confess to their father the crime and deceit of the past. They would see that the present good radiated the power of God.

13. *And he fell upon his brother Benjamin's neck, and wept.* These were tears of joy. Indeed, humility cherishes the tender feelings.

14. *After that his brethren talked with him.* They were now at rest, the past forgiven, the present full of hope, and they could now tell Joseph the many things he wished to know about them and to learn Joseph's history from him, that they might repeat the marvelous tale to their father.

Gospel Applications (1) We have a Prince, a King, holding all riches in His power, and we should tell others. (2) When God invites us to come, it is to abide in His kingdom, and eat of the richness of His blessings. (3) There is the perfect assurance of forgiveness. (4) God brings good out of evil, and teaches us, as we look at the depth of our sins, to see the height of His love and to wonder and adore so wondrous a salvation. (5) Christ expresses His love to us. He loads us with kindness. He rejoices with us. (6) We talk with Him now as His children, read His Word and walk in loving communion with Him.

Practical Observations in Conclusion

1. Much of the punishment of all sin is future punishment, Joseph's brethren were suffering for sins committed twenty-two years before.

2. Those who have done wrong must expect to be tested and proved before they are received back into friendship and trust.

3. Often times it is by some circumstance or event, which perplexes, troubles, or gladdens us that leads to new thoughts regarding conduct and communicate important ideas for success in life.

4. In finding their lost brother again, the sons of Jacob also found their own better selves which they had lost. They had been living in a lie, unable to look the past in the face.

5. Your only protection against ruin through exposure is in refraining from sin, which will always expose you.

6. Note the delicacy and courtesy with which Joseph treated his brothers who had injured him. These are basic Christian virtues to be diligently cultivated that lead to success.

7. There is great comfort and encouragement in the assurance that God overrules all. He does not destroy man's free-will, but He uses man's actions to accomplish His own purposes. What a sad and hopeless thing it would be if the world of human affairs were like the chance world of "Hafed's Dream!" Looking for an acre of diamonds, Hafed lost what was really valuable. The Lord reigneth. The Lord, infinite in wisdom, love, and power, is our basis for being overcomers.

Chapter Twelve

Success

In all thy ways acknowledge him,
and he shall direct thy paths. Proverbs 3:6

Trusting God, emotional balance, and success go hand-in-hand. Working according to God's plan, believers can indeed become extraordinary overcomers!

When speaking of lasting success we are referring primarily to the eternal inheritance of heaven that God provides to believers. There are merging factors, however, that cause God to bless the activities of the faithful during their earthly pilgrimage, and we have the duty to do our best while we are here. The blessing of forgiven sin and direction from the Holy Spirit cost us nothing. For God, though, the price was very costly. The mandate for doing our best goes back to the beginnings when God said, "Be fruitful, and multiply, and replenish the earth, and subdue it: and have dominion . . ." (Genesis 1:28).

If through the years we have been storing in our minds the world's way of thinking, then our souls are surely darkened. God can only give light and remove the chaff when Christians search His Word. He "is able to do exceeding abundantly above all that we ask or think, according to the power that worketh in us," so that we can "comprehend with all saints what is the breadth, and length, and depth, and height; And to know the love of Christ, which passeth knowledge, that we might be filled with all the fullness of God" (Ephesians 3:18-20).

God's Plan for Success:

1. Recognize that God's Word is true and practical in all matters. The principles for success are taught in Proverbs 2:1-11. Our desire should be to have the ability to see each situation, to know the ramifications of the options available, and to make the choices that will give the best outcome. When God and His Word are our number one priority, we will "be filled with the knowledge of his will" (Colossians 1:9b).

> Successful people are not double-minded. When we have the mind of God through Christ, our mind then serves as a marvelous discerner. The consequences of the alternatives become apparent and good decisions can be made.

2. Have a challenging goal in mind. My friend's goal to be a dentist, mentioned in chapter eight, was an important first step in the chain of success. A goal, however, is only legitimate if it meets a vital stipulation: *will it bring honor to God?*

> One time a man asked me if I was the guy who had retired by age 50. I answered, "Yes, but that was not my goal!" Why was it not my goal? Because it was not a proper priority. If it happened, it happened; but if that achievement had been paramount in my life, I would have failed to achieve three far more important goals. I would have failed to be in fellowship with God, I would have ruined my marriage, and I would have failed my children. The battle of overcoming the problems associated with high goals is God's, not ours. "But rather seek ye the kingdom of God; and all these things shall be added unto you" (Luke 12:31).

> Do not be afraid to break free from the past. It is important that we uncover and reject the imprisonment caused by feelings of inferiority. Ethel Waters had it right—"My daddy told me that God don't make no

mistakes." It is important that our goals be realistic. With God's help, we can look to the accomplishments of others to find and adopt goals that blend with our own talents.

Success involves both leadership and followers or what could be described as responsible leadership support. Leadership means being in control where you are responsible, and maintaining the initiative according to God's Word. Leaders find true happiness in serving others and are accessible. Leadership involves getting people to do the right thing because they want to. Success never arises from tolerance for half-truth or half-effort. Successful leadership also requires accountability and a willingness to learn from one's own mistakes. This is where leadership support becomes especially beneficial. It is important to have others around who will caringly expose a leader's mistakes to him in private.

Humility and a fixed focus are two characteristics of servant leaders who excel. If you are walking with God and have learned to be a supportive and loving spouse, you are already a success. If you are succeeding as parents in building character and discipline into the lives of your children, you are already a big success!

3. Consciously place a high value on your time and goals. We avoid wasting time by avoiding bad decisions. God helps us see to it that His first choice for our lives is also our first choice: "This book of the law [rules for success] shall not depart out of thy mouth; but thou shalt meditate therein day and night, that thou mayest observe to do according to all that is written therein: for then thou shalt make thy way prosperous, and then thou shalt have good success" (Joshua 1:8).

Success in managing one's emotions brings personal joy and God's power needed to succeed—two characteristics that become readily apparent to others. "Meditate upon these things; give thyself wholly to them [for God's glory]; that thy profiting may appear to all" (I Timothy 4:15).

"When wisdom entereth into thine heart, and knowledge is pleasant unto thy soul; Discretion shall preserve thee, understanding shall keep thee" (Proverbs 2:10-11). Discretion is the capacity to choose from many options the one that will give the best result. *"Blessed is the man that walketh not in the counsel of the ungodly* [but instead with the righteous], *nor standeth in the way of* [with] *sinners, nor sitteth in the seat of the scornful. But his delight is in the law of the LORD; and in his law doth he meditate day and night. And he shall be like a tree planted by the rivers of water, that bringeth forth his fruit in his season; his leaf also shall not wither; and whatsoever he doeth shall prosper"* (Psalm 1:1-3). These ideas for our success are dependable because they are God's!

4. Understand Step-by-Step What Is Needed to Achieve the Goal. Reaching extraordinary goals involves study, thinking, planning, and action. Every profession, mission, and trade requires an awareness of and concentration on the steps, such as those listed in this chapter, which are helpful in order to succeed. Take no shortcuts. Build on a solid foundation. (See common traits of good leadership, page 4.)

Success follows clearly within the boundaries of Bible doctrine. Obedience to God's Word gives understanding: "He keepeth the paths of judgment, and preserveth the way of his saints. Then shalt thou understand righteousness, and judgment [consequences of options available], and equity; yea, every good path" (Proverbs 2:8-9). David, who had pridefully numbered Israel and had a sordid affair, got right with God! After a soul-wrenching repentance, he started all over again and became a man after God's own heart." "O how love I thy law! it is my meditation all the day. Thou through thy commandments hast made me wiser than mine enemies: for they are ever with me. I understand more than the ancients, because I keep thy precepts" (Psalms 119:97-98, 100).

We want God's will. It is very important to maintain a to-do list (prayer list) of needs requiring a solution and to re-prioritize this list daily. Fellowship with God is the link that empowers the divine God-to-man co-operative. Biographies of achievers always include a continuous series of obstacles that had to be overcome in order to reach goals. We want God's opinion on how to overcome barriers; that way, we will not have to keep trying to solve the same problems over and over again.

Storing truth in our minds is the fundamental key to success. Whatever your goals may be, continually think about them in a positive way. Study God's Word and ask Him for wisdom. The principal point is expressed in Proverbs 2:1a: "My son, if thou wilt receive my words." Receiving God's Word means having the truth engrafted into one's subconscious values library (attitude). This "receiving"—storing a new conviction—was what I was unconsciously doing when advising my friend about becoming a dentist. Storing (believing) in my own mind the words I was using to convince him changed my own attitude, goals, and life (See pages 59 and 62).

5. Reckon the goal to be accomplished. Proceed with unwavering conviction, step-by-step, doing what needs to be done. Our time is very valuable, of course, and some obstacles will arise that are not worth our time. Faith in God's provision generates ongoing determination. "He [God] layeth up sound wisdom for the righteous: he is a buckler to them that walk uprightly" (Proverbs 2:7).

The cost of mediocrity is much higher than the price in commitment and work associated with success. Once, when addressing students at an elite school in England, Winston Churchill gave the following exhortation: "Never give up; never, never give up; never, never, never give up." He then concluded by saying, "Never give up," and left the room. This principle is important to remember because considerable time usually passes before success becomes apparent. The testimony of extraordinary achievement always presents a continual succession of difficulties. God usually does one of three things. He may guide you around the difficulty, remove the difficulty, or give you a new and better goal.

One of the obstacles I encountered when starting my business was opposition from a club of three real estate company owners who conspired to keep new competitors out of the real estate marketing business. I had started an insurance agency, and it had quickly became apparent that realtors were taking homeowner insurance clients away from me. It then seemed wise for me to become a realtor too.

By God's providence, I went to a good man who patiently taught me real estate law. This man was not a part of that club. I then took the state exam and put up a real estate company sign. All of a sudden a battle I had not expected was on!

The club invited me to meet with them, and they sought to assure me that I would fail. The club's biggest hindrance to my progress as a real estate broker was their rule restricting competition. I was limited to hiring only salespeople who were the primary wage earners in their families. For a beginning company, that was an impossible hurdle.

The threats of the club had two consequences. I became filled with determination, and, contrary to my original plan, I decided to de-emphasize insurance and build a substantial real estate sales company.

God is always there to help you when you have a righteous cause. To make a long story short, by God's direction, within two years there was an anti-monopoly bill before the Iowa legislature. The Iowa Association of Realtors notified our local board that if they did not get off Dave Norris' back, they would be expelled from the Association.

At the next meeting of the local real estate company owners, they were informed of the Iowa Association's ruling, and the local board president said, "This is all because of that doggoned Dave Norris!"

After informing the members of the ruling, the president asked me if I would like to make the motion to change the rule. I answered, "No, I'm going to obey the rules; if you want to change the rule, that's fine with me."

Within a few years, these same men elected me to be their president. We were able to usher the entire business community through rather odious crises. At that time, the editor of the local newspaper had turned it into an anti-business, anti-free-enterprise publication. With the support of another company owner, Chuck Gray, I convinced the real estate company owners to quit advertising in the paper and to tell the community why. When we were voting on the matter, one of the realtors argued that we had no right to dictate what the editor was to do. I assured him that he was right but that, by the same principle, the newspaper had no right to tell us where to spend our advertising dollars. Within about four weeks I received assurances that the editor had changed his mind. Apparently, he had decided that respecting the work of the Ames, Iowa, business community had some merit after all.

After I retired, the man who had taught me real estate law, Larry Baldus, spotted my family at a local restaurant. He came over to chat, and in the course of the conversation he said, "Norris, one thing I remember about you—you always sat next to your enemies (those conspiring to keep me down) when we had those meetings." That, of course, is the work of God upon the heart and emotions of a sinner saved by grace.

Success is the ultimate reward for those who continually acknowledge God. "Trust in the LORD with all thine heart; and lean not unto thine own understanding. In all thy ways acknowledge him, and he shall direct thy paths" (Proverbs 3:5-6).

BONUS BOOK

FOR
THE FAMILY

FOR
THE FAMILY

Your Acre of Diamonds

David A. Norris

Alpha Heartland Press • Ames, Iowa

CONTENTS

—

DEDICATION

This book is dedicated to our three daughters
Susan, Sharon, and Sara
whose teaching ministries
are appreciated and have been a source of great joy

ACKNOWLEDGMENTS

Thank you to Ruth Myers for her outline on the family. Ruth and her husband Warren spent a lifetime as missionaries in Southeast Asia. Before our daughters were grown and gone and our memories of what seemed to work in parenting had faded, Carlene and I wrote chapters one and two. We built upon Ruth's outline.

Clark R. Bowers is also appreciated for his research into public school curriculum as it is today. Major changes have occurred in primary and secondary education since my exposure to the subject when chairing the Grand Jury in Iowa (chapter four).

The following two publications are recommended for further reading: a history book, *The Myth of Separation,* by David Barton, WallBuilder Press, Aledo, Texas; and *Understanding the Times* by David A. Noebel, Harvest House Publishers, Eugene, Oregon.

Hamilton A. Long has done an excellent job of extrapolating and authenticating American principles taken from Judeo-Christian theism, *Your American Yardstick*, Your Heritage Books, Inc., Philadelphia, Pennsylvania, 1963.

Liberty Fund Inc. markets excellent books tracing the development of responsible liberty and problem alerts built into the founding documents for American law. Liberty Fund Books, 8335 Allison Pointe Trail, #300, Indianapolis, Indiana.

Chapter One

Who's Who in the Home and Parental Unity

And the rib, which the LORD God had taken
from man, made he a woman, and brought her
unto the man. Genesis 2:22

The Family Is God's Institution:

• "A family is a deeply-rooted tree with branches of different strength all receiving nourishment from an infinite source.
• A family is where truth is learned, character is formed, ethics are practiced and society is preserved.
• A family is where all members contribute and share, cooperate and work and accept their responsibilities toward each other.
• A family is where holidays are celebrated with feasting, birthdays acknowledged with gifts, and thoughts of days gone by are kept alive with fond remembrances.
• A family is where each can find solace and comfort in grief, pleasure and laughter in joy, and kindness and encouragement in daily living.
• A family is a haven of rest, a sanctuary of peace and most of all, a harbor of love."

Author Unknown

[1]

Biblical guidelines for the family stand in total contrast to the secular worldview. The family begins with a man and a woman living faithfully together in marriage for life. They nurture and rear their children to respect God's Word. The educational systems and religions based on secular humanism, liberalism and the new age movement are enemies of the family. Their false teachings strive to dissolve the solidarity of the family. Children become the wards of a paternal and exploitive hierarchy or state.

Happy families are the products of a living faith in God's Word. "Through wisdom is an house builded; and by understanding it is established" (Proverbs 24:3).

When proceeding according to Biblical guidelines, the husband and wife are committed to each other, and they complement one another. Their roles, equally important, are neither identical nor interchangeable. Together they can accomplish far more than they could on their own.

The marriage that ignores God is in conflict with creation. Some of the greatest problems in the home can be traced to the husband's failure to be a spiritual leader. There is no security when the husband is bossy or, at the other extreme, neutral in all matters. In I Samuel 13:13-14 and 15:28, we can see how a parent's failure caused his children to lose their heritage.

I. The Husband and Wife See Things Differently

When we study the emotional differences between men and women, the advantages God affords in marriage become apparent. Men tend to overlook important matters and to be too optimistic. We could compare the husband to the positive post of a car battery. The wife, on the other hand, with sensitivity to detail, tends to be negative. When we make a direct connection between the negative and positive posts of a battery, sparks fly. The way to avoid this is to have a converter between the two posts which will turn the conflict of strong positives and negatives into constructive power. See chapter two of *Lasting Success*, pages 17 and 18.

Communication, affection, appreciation, and reverence toward one another in marriage are the products of a Christ-like spirit. Members of a happy family are dedicated to promoting one another's welfare—Ephesians 5:33.

The family is of immeasurable value to happiness and life's fulfillment. This is illustrated by Russell Conwell's *Acre of Diamonds*. The story, set in Persia in the late 1870s, is about a farmer named Ali Hafed.

> Ali Hafed owned a very large farm with grain fields and orchards. He was a wealthy and contented man. One day when he was in the marketplace, he was told about an acre of diamonds which was situated between two mountains. Not understanding that emotional highs must be abated, the thought of an acre of diamonds made him feel poor. Driven by this, Ali began a search for the acre of diamonds. To finance the endeavor, he eventually sold the farm that had prospered him and his family. In time, he lost his family and his health. Later, when he was a totally broken man, the news came—others had found the acre of diamonds. They found the diamonds on the farm he had sold.

Those who are wise and alert do not neglect what really counts. The family is our acre of diamonds!

II. The Husband's Function and Nature
The husband's function is that of leader, protector, and provider. Men have a hero instinct and need to have their role appreciated. Knowing God's Word is the key to leadership in the home. Becoming a good leader in the home provides experience that is important for successful leadership outside the home.

The husband's role and responsibility toward his wife:
1. "Likewise, ye husbands, dwell with them according to knowledge . . ." I Peter 3:7a. The roles of husband and wife are equally important, but each is superior in specific ways. It is important that the husband have empathy for the fact that his wife is, in an emotional and

physical sense, the weaker vessel. Christ gave His life for the church. We are to care for our wives as Christ cares for the church: "For the husband is the head of the wife, even as Christ is the head of the church: and he is the saviour of the body," Ephesians 5:23. The husband is to assure his wife that she is the most important and loved person on earth.

2. The husband is to encourage his wife to have satisfaction in her role by admiring her work and accomplishments. In a normal marriage, the husband is content and feels loved. This is not always true with the wife. The husband needs to reach beyond his comfort zone, paying special attention to and communicating with his wife. This is an everyday responsibility and means putting aside all thoughts about projects or reading the newspaper. The husband should be interested in knowing how his wife's day went. He needs to look her in the eye and encourage her to share her thoughts and concerns.

3. The husband is to be the backbone of consistent discipline of his children.

4. The husband is the head of the home, but in the decision process he needs to consult his wife. God is the Boss! The husband is an undershepherd, the final arbitrator of policies and decisions impacting his family.

5. The husband is to help the home atmosphere by being positive and cheerful. He can help by turning the periodic kitchen disaster for his wife into a show of love. "A merry heart doeth good like a medicine . . ." Proverbs 17:22a.

6. The Bible says a husband should:
Not leave his wife, though she is unbelieving—
    I Corinthians 7:11-12, 14, 16.
Not interfere with his wife's duties to Christ—
    Luke 14:26.

The Duties of a Husband to His Wife:
- To be faithful to her—Proverbs 5:19; Malachi 2:14-15
- To comfort her—I Samuel 1:8
- To consult her—Genesis 31:4-7
- To dwell with her for life—Genesis 2:24; Matthew 19:3-9

- To have only one wife—Genesis 2:24; Mark 10:6-8
- To love her—Ephesians 5:25; Colossians 3:19
- To regard her as himself—Genesis 2:23; Matthew 19:5
- To respect her—I Peter 3:7

III. The Wife's Function and Needs

As the bearer and nurturer of her children, the wife desires a secure home environment. She needs identity and love. "Whoso findeth a wife findeth a good thing, and obtaineth favour of the LORD" (Proverbs 18:22). We are told, "That they [experienced women] may teach the young women to be sober [wise], to love their husbands, to love their children, to be discreet, chaste, keepers at home, good, obedient to their own husbands, that the word of God be not blasphemed [irreverenced]" (Titus 2:4-5).

The demonstration of love between parents is very important to the development of their children. A daughter tends to treat her husband the same way her mother treated her father.

The wife's role and responsibility to her husband:
1. The wife is to promote a dynamic leader. She must be careful to stay under his authority (Genesis 2:18). The wife is to be a "help" suitable for her husband (Genesis 2:18). Proverbs 31:10-31 presents a beautiful picture of the role of a happy wife. The wife's role as a leadership-support person is extremely well defined in the Bible: "Wives, submit yourselves unto your own husbands, as unto the Lord" (Ephesians 5:22).

2. The wife is to guard her tongue for the safety of the children as well as her own soul. Youngsters find it difficult to see their own sin, but they can spot ours in a minute. Gossip drives children away from Biblical authority, into the arms of Satan.

3. The wife is to support her husband in his work by her attitude. She should be grateful and let him know he is appreciated for his leadership (Ephesians 5:22-24; I Peter 3:1-4).

4. The wife is to love and respect her husband even if she disagrees with him. She should appeal to him for improvement in private. We all make mistakes. God knew this when He established our respective roles. Wise men learn from the insights their wives share with them. The manner in which husbands and wives submit to their God-given roles is the example that the children will follow.

Good is exemplified: Isaac, Genesis 24:67; Elkanah,
    I Samuel 1:3-5.
Bad is exemplified: Solomon, I Kings 11:1; Ahasuerus,
    Esther 1:10-11.

5. The Bible says to wives:
Leadership of the husband in the home was established before the fall of mankind in the Garden of Eden. God allows no substitutes. A wife should not embarrass her husband by challenging his judgment in public. Not only can this crush a man's incentive to lead, but it also violates God's plan for who's who in the home.

The duties of a wife to her husband:
- To allow him to be the family spokesman in
    controversial matters—I Corinthians 14:34
- To be faithful to him—I Corinthians 7:3-5, 10
- To be subject to him—Genesis 3:16; Ephesians 5:22-24;
    I Peter 3:1; I Corinthians 14:34; Titus 2:5
- To bring honor to him—Proverbs 31:23, 28
- To love him—Titus 2:4
- To remain with him for life—Romans 7:2-3
- To secure his confidence—Proverbs 31:11

Wives should be adorned:
- With modesty and sobriety—I Timothy 2:9
- With a meek and quiet spirit—I Peter 3:4-5
- With good works—I Timothy 2:10; 5:10
- With diligence and prudence—Proverbs 31:13-27
- With benevolence to the poor—Proverbs 31:20
- With a sense of duty to unbelieving husbands—
    I Corinthians 7:13-14, 16; I Peter 3:1-2

Good is exemplified by Ruth—Ruth 1:4; and Priscilla—Acts 18:2, 26.
Bad is exemplified by Samson's wife—Judges 14:15-17; Michal—II Samuel 6:16; and Jesebel—I Kings 21:25.

IV. There Should Be Unity in the Presence of the Children

God is the Head of the home. God runs the home with the father's help as undershepherd and the mother's help as his assistant.

"For I know him [Abraham], that he will command his children and his household after him, and they shall keep the way of the LORD, to do justice and judgment . . ." (Genesis 18:19).

"She looketh well to the ways of her household [parental unity], and eateth not the bread of idleness. Her children arise up, and call her blessed; her husband also, and he praiseth her" (Proverbs 31:27-28).

1. Avoid marital strife around children.
2. Be consistent with each other in child discipline and punish authority-jumping (the child is told "No" by one parent and then goes to the other to get permission).
3. Treat children impartially.
4. Balance jealousy among older children with impartial love, lest the older child's subconscious values become fixed against the parents.
5. Avoid favoritism toward older children; it can give younger children an inferior self-image.
6. Never tolerate a child's disrespect toward the other parent.

TOPICS FOR TEAM DISCUSSION

1. Does your wife know she is loved? (Ephesians 5:25) - - -
2. Family devotions / Bible reading / prayer - - - - - - - - - -
3. Do you communicate and consult with each other? - - - -

4. Honesty and follow-through with children and others - -
5. Church, Sunday school, midweek service attendance - - -
6. Husband promoting a cheerful home atmosphere - - - - -
7. Tolerating no abuse or disrespect toward mother - - - - - -
8. Parental harmony in the presence of the children - - - - - -
9. Knowing children personally, how they differ - - - - - - - -
10. Consistency with rules and discipline of children - - - - - -
11. Husband as the backbone for discipline of children -- - - -
12. Are music and literature used wholesome? - - - - - - - - --
13. Wholesome entertainment, TV properly limited - - - - - -
14. Implementation of a good dating policy for teens - - - - - -
15. Importance of Matthew 18 taught and practiced - - - - - - -
16. Monitor and control of children's associations - - - - - - - -
17. Both parents spending quality time with family - - - - - - -
18. Demonstration of respect for the role God has given to authority persons -
19. Practicing thrift with finances, tithing regularly - - - - - - -
20. Other topics for team discussion - - - - - - - - - - - - - - - - -

Sharing Ideas – How Can We Improve?

What are some God-honoring things that you as a woman would like to see come to pass?

Are you sensitive to your mate's needs? Are there things you can do that would give her/him renewed joy as a wife/husband?

What do you see that you would consider doing differently if you were the husband/leader?

What would you consider doing differently if you were the wife/helpmeet?

Am I allowing you enough opportunity to be the woman God would have you to be?

What are some of your thoughts and goals for the children, for the family?

What are some of your fears, hurts?

If God suddenly took either of us to glory, how would the surviving spouse manage financially and otherwise? Are we realistic about things that will impact our future?

Conclusion

It takes work to have a strong, happy family. We need to be sensitive to the roles God has given us as partners in marriage.

If the woman is unsubmissive and the man is strong-willed, there will be conflict in the marriage.

If the woman is unsubmissive and the man is acquiescent, the marriage will also be troubled. This is also a harmful example for the children. The wife's dominance in the home will likely mean trouble in the church.

If the woman is in submission and the man is a thoughtful husband, the woman, the man, and their marriage will be great.

As love and transparency deepen, an appreciation for the unique gifts and roles of each partner grows. The marriage excels!

"The law of the LORD is perfect, converting the soul [mind, will, and emotion]: the testimony of the LORD is sure, making wise the simple [gives us understanding]. The statutes of the LORD are right, rejoicing the heart: the commandment of the LORD is pure, enlightening the eyes. The fear of the LORD is clean, enduring for ever: the judgments of the LORD are true and righteous altogether. More to be desired are they than gold, yea, than much fine gold: sweeter also than honey and the honeycomb" (Psalm 19:7-10).

Chapter Two

Parent - Child Relationships

That men may know that thou, whose name alone is
JEHOVAH, art the most high over all the earth. Psalm 83:18
Bring them up in the nurture and admonition of the Lord.
Ephesians 6:4b

Military historians focus on the locations where great
weapons of war were put to work and decisive battles were
fought. The basis for victory over the enemies of our
children and civilized culture is summarized in the verses
above. Parents have an indispensable role in taming
rebellion and building character in the attitudes of their
children. If parents neglect this role, their children can grow
up to be defenseless casualties of "feel good" emotions and
the deceptive promises of a godless world.

Parents can also harm their children's future by indulging in
a self-satisfying and delusional view of love. Yielding to the
determined will of little ones is not love. Instead, it ignores
the kind of world which the children must be prepared to
face. Children can not learn to set misleading emotions aside
without parental instruction, controls, and supervision. As
objectionable as it may seem to some, this message of
genuine love (parental responsibility) should start on day
one in the life of a child.

Babies are smarter than some parents realize. Babies are to be loved and cuddled, but to pick them up every time they cry suggests that the baby is in command and sends the wrong message. A crying spell that has no connection to need (such as sickness, hunger, or a diaper problem) is good for their health. It is far better for the child to experience genuine parenting than to be spoiled (motivated by untamed emotions), and when older to suffer exploitation by the world.

Some children who were not disciplined at home will later realize that feeling-based decisions can not be trusted, and they will come to regret the fact that much of their life has been wasted.

The following are three examples of emotional immaturity in parents that cause them to be permissive of rebellion by their children:

A. The attitude that "this is my child, and I have a right to pamper my child" can be very harmful. Such self-indulgence blinds parents to the destructive influence of permissiveness that will eventually come to haunt the life of a self-willed child.

B. Emotional factors lead some parents away from the fact that the issue between them and the child is, in fact, emotions. Successful parenting is a direct confrontation between (1) the will of parents who should be emotionally mature and (2) the immature but determined will of the child. Wise parents know that God's Word has the answers to life, and they must exercise control at times over their child's choices. When parents fail in this area, their child will not learn to superintend his or her feelings and make reliable choices.

C. Parents may foster rebellion by pampering their child because they fear that the child will not love them. But the opposite usually happens. Parents almost always lose the respect of their children when they do not exercise authority with clarity.

Many parents want to train up their children to be responsible citizens, but they simply do not know how. Children need to be taught that good decisions are based upon a rational evaluation of predictable outcomes which may have nothing to do with feelings. This should be accomplished by the time they are confronted with peer pressure and sexual drives, which are the subject of this chapter.

The words of the father and mother are the rule of conduct (law) for their children (Exodus 20:12). As God's agents, parents communicate approval and disapproval: "Afterward it [chastisement] yieldeth the peaceable fruit of righteousness unto them which are exercised thereby" (Hebrews 12:11b). Parents provide a pilot plant version of the larger consequences that befall foolish adult behavior (Psalm 51:8). Parents help children to understand and hate sin (I Corinthians 11:31).

I.   Let God Lead— Be Accountable As a Parent

"And these words, which I command thee this day, shall be in thine heart: And thou shalt teach them diligently unto thy children, and shalt talk of them when thou sittest in thine house, and when thou walkest by the way, and when thou liest down, and when thou risest up" (Deuteronomy 6:6-7).

It is not possible to teach a child until he or she is first brought under control.

   A. God has given parents the authority and responsibility to lovingly superintend their children.
   • The idea that parents are not able to control their children is untrue. As babies, we put up a storm in the attempt to control our parents; we should certainly be stronger now as adults than we were as children.

- Single men are wise to have an understanding with their potential bride that the husband is the leader in the home. They must then be sure to be humble and loving leaders.
- The husband should be the spiritual leader in his home and the backbone for discipline. No disrespect by the children toward their mother is to be tolerated (Hebrews 12:9-11; I Timothy 2:12).
- Children need a father and mother who care enough about them to be consistent and exercise tough love.
- First-time parents should find out what problems other parents have encountered and be prepared in advance, because they will face the same problems.
- Parents who know Christ gain understanding from the Bible and the indwelling Holy Spirit for the **how**, **when**, and **how much** that are needed for parenting.
- Parents are not perfect, but they are to do their best and exercise authority under God (Ephesians 6:1).
- Daily family devotions which are not overly long or complicated are important. **However, being consistent in our daily walk and parenting says more than anything else we say or do**.
- Consistent parental exercise of godly authority for discipline helps children understand the consequences of rebellion and accountability to God.
- Parents should do all they can to lead their little ones to Christ. This means quality time, family togetherness, devotions, church, Sunday school, and Christian youth activities. **When praying aloud during family devotions, praying that the children will accept Christ at an early age is of great value**.
- The lack of understanding among young parents calls for a formal parent-training ministry, such as that outlined here, for young married couples in our churches.

B. Parenting is not for cowards.
- Children come into this world rebellious and untamed. From the Bible and from firsthand observation we know that children go astray from birth and will soon be "speaking lies" (Psalm 58:3).
- Parenting involves a contest of wills. You can not be successful as a parent until you recognize this truth.
- From the day babies are born, they have their antennae out to test their parents. They want to see if their parents are determined enough to be in control. Satan is in there trying to give parents a guilt trip for being in charge.
- Parents who discipline inappropriate behavior and build character into the lives of their children stand in Satan's way. Satan hates children because of their spiritual potential for right living.
- The child nurtured by love, teachable observations, and firmness will rise above the crowd in character to a status of strong, self-assured, moral individualism (Deuteronomy 6:6-7; Proverbs 3:1-7).

C. There is no substitute for the exercise of parental authority!
- For their own good, children should not be allowed to function under the control of their sinful nature.
- We should not worry about whether or not a child loves us. When we do the job God expects, He sees to it that our children respect us.
- Without the controlling help of parents, the strong sin-laden emotions within a child will not be brought under control.
- The church is supportive, but it can not fill the parents' role. Christian schools help, but they can not do what parents must do.
- Children respect guidelines, and they disrespect weakness. This instinct makes them want to know how strong mom and dad are. Occasionally they will disobey just to determine whether there has been any change.

- The price of being a parental wimp is ending up with a child who does not have enough emotional maturity and self-discipline to avoid cheap relationships, drugs, and immorality (Proverbs 10:1b; 17:21; 29:15b).
- Insofar as parental success is concerned, the price of involvement is not nearly as high as that of failure.

D. Parental accountability brings great blessings.
  - The joy that comes from exercising parental authority is the fulfillment of God's promise—that it may be well in the life of our children and that they may live long and fruitful lives on this earth (Ephesians 6:2-3).
  - Another added benefit of parental accountability is the blessing which ordered and successful lives bring to the church, society, and future generations (Proverbs 17:6; 29:17; Malachi 2:15).

II. Listen— Be Their Trusted Confidant

- Teach the children that friends can not be trusted with secrets.
- Do not overreact when your children say things you do not like. It is better to correct them gradually than to discourage them from talking.
- Be an understanding sponge; be their encourager; be sure that you, the parent, are there when they get home from school. **If the mother can handle it, home schooling is best**. There are several companies which provide excellent textbooks and teacher guides for home schooling.
- When a happening occurs, large or small, fun or sad, be there and listen, listen, listen. Listening helps keep them close.

III. Learn—Spend Quality Time With Them—Know Them

- Observe their attributes, their tendencies, what is normal and what is not (Psalm 51:5; I Peter 3:7).

- Know what they are saying by their body language and what they are saying when you are not around.
- Precede disincentives which are appropriate for their misbehavior with **a clear explanation of the offense**. Given the opportunity, Satan will take advantage of any confusion and turn the child's mind to self-righteousness and parent-condemnation (Proverbs 16:18; Hebrews 12:15). "And, ye fathers, provoke not your children to wrath: but bring them up in the nurture and admonition of the Lord" (Ephesians 6:4).
- Do not push them to self-doubt. Distinguish between willful disobedience and an inability to perform due to immaturity. Youthful inability can usually be handled through a time of show-and-tell, and sometimes responsibilities should be less intensive.
- Administer discipline in love. Children will test their parents, but will usually submit with respect to this kind of discipline.

IV. Love—God Says We Are to Love Our Children (Titus 2:4)

Parents who fail to understand a child's perception of love demonstrated by parental guidelines fail miserably. Demonstrations of love such as the following are important for preventing a generation gap:

A. As father and mother, show love toward one another.
B. Provide a secure home; handle parental differences in private.
- In God's order parents work as a team, with the father as the head of the home. Children are created to respond to this arrangement. The practice of this biblical concept is an emotional stabilizer, a benefit of obedience to God's chain of authority.

C. Frequently tell your children you love them. Show your love often with a kiss, a hug, and a loving touch.
D. Tell them that even though you love them, God loves them even more.
  - Tell them that you are not perfect, and, in the final analysis, we are all accountable to God. When you realize you have made a mistake, apologize, but do not relinquish your duty to be the parent.
  - To save children from themselves, from the world, and from Satan, hold firmly to boundaries for behavior and practice in an attitude of love! When a parent says "No!" it means no! God requires discipline, children need it, and they will thank you for it later (Hebrews 12:11).
E. Know where they are at all times; this is a very important aspect of love.
  - We have had years of adult experience. Children are without this, and God has called us to be their safety net. The at-home mother has a special advantage in monitoring her children's activity (Proverbs 31:27-28).
  - Have their friends in your home where you can observe them firsthand. Children's activities go forward with your advice and consent.
  - Someday, when they are a little older and chafing under your dating policy, they may say, "Dad, you don't trust me!" The answer is, "I trust you, but I don't trust your biology. I don't even trust my own biology, so I also must exercise care about my activities."
  - Have a definite time established for children to check in or return home. They may not admit it, but children understand this restriction as a demonstration of parental love.
F. Respect their God-given individuality and their property.
G. **Do not spoil them. Give them responsibilities and teach them to work in order to acquire things.**

H. **Read to the children, beginning when they are very young. This activity creates in them the desire to learn to read**.

I. Help by explaining the nature of peer pressure before it seeks to control them.
   - Even in Christian circles, peer pressure bent on evil exists among children. It seeks to establish and enforce worldly standards for language, music, dress, and dating that are carnal and sensual.
   - Establish and enforce reasonable standards (parameters) that clearly set the children apart from the world's relationships, dress, music, *et cetera*. When they realize they can stand alone, they become strong as individuals.

J. Make them feel wanted and important in the home.
   - Treat them with respect. Bring them (with some counsel) into big decisions, such as purchasing a new car, choosing a vacation, *et cetera*.

K. Compliment their good actions.
   - Teach by observing their talents, and support them with praise and the tools needed to promote their development.

V. Lead!

Teach them obedience to a reasonable set of standards for behavior. This is a most important by-product of genuine parental love. "A child left to himself bringeth his mother to shame" (Proverbs 29:15b).

- Do not condone a temper. Doing so strengthens their wicked nature and resolve to have control.
- Learning can not even begin until you have children under control. Get them under control when they are young, and discipline will be much less of a problem as they grow older (Proverbs 23-25).
- Do not gossip. They may not see their own mistakes, but they identify the evil of gossip which in turn leads to disrespect for the gossiping parent.

- If children are in trouble with the teacher, they should be in trouble with dad. If you do not trust the teacher, get them into a different school.
- Eliminate confusion—do not have too many rules. Clearly identify what is expected and be consistent. Parents should not tolerate the need to repeat a command again and again (Deuteronomy 6:7-9).
- If children do not learn at home under forthright parents, they will learn in later years under the cruel hand of the world.
- "He that spareth his rod hateth his son: but he that loveth him chasteneth him betimes" (Proverbs 13:24).
- When children deliberately disobey, do not show anger or fear; calmly accept the challenge and win—decisively.
- Disincentives, such as the removal of privileges, can be effective.
- Do not give up. Love hangs in there, and the child will eventually settle down.

VI. Dating Policy—A Must!

Dating is a serious matter with lifetime consequences. "A youth boiling with hormones will wonder why he should not give full freedom to his sexual desires. If he is unchecked by custom, morals or laws, he may ruin his life before he matures sufficiently to understand that sex is a river of fire that must be banked and cooled by a hundred restraints if it is not to consume in chaos both the individual and the group." (From a summary of *The Lessons of History* by Will and Ariel Durant, printed in *The Readers Digest*, December 1968. *The Lessons of History* is a study of twenty civilizations throughout 4,000 years of history and was hailed by the historian Allan Nevins as "one of the outstanding works of American historiography.")

"See then [parents and others] that ye walk circumspectly, not as fools, but as wise, redeeming the time, because the days are evil" (Ephesians 5:15-16).

Although we should be concerned about the world's children, this book is not about them. We are concerned here about the devastation among young people from Christian homes. We are losing them by the tens of thousands.

An anti-American, anti-Judeo-Christian, no-boundaries premise for curriculum has been forced upon many public schools. Tenure guarantees imposed by teachers' unions leave school administrators powerless to prevent moral pollution by a few secular humanist teachers. Joined by the leftist media, these teachers look upon moral authority with disrespect and insist that foul language, promiscuous sex, addictive drugs, and unwed mothers to be considered the norm.

- This insidious scourge upon our youth, our homes, the church, and God's name can be stopped (I John 4:4; Isaiah 43:2).

- It is in the interest of all people who love America and liberty to support and promote God-honoring education. We have a duty to support one another and encourage Bible-based parent training. This includes lovingly helping unsettled families and single parents to be sure that their young people do not slip through the cracks.

> Failure to enforce a family dating policy that assures an emotionally balanced dating sequence leaves the child very vulnerable to sexual sin.

- A well-thought-out dating policy gives parents an upper hand in the war with Satan and his hosts. It is up to parents to determine what that policy will be and then to see to it that it is followed. Poor parent-image is manifested by the parents' reluctance to discipline and to enforce compliance with family policy.

- When the parents lose control, they lose respect. The child loses both confidence in the parents and the security that goes with it.
- The loss of just one precious young person to a weak marriage is a big loss to the family, the church, the community, and our nation. It is the peace and contentment of a happy marriage which frees energies and time for a fruitful life.

Sample Dating Policy

A. Date Christians only—those who are spiritual, money-wise, and industrious. Learning to evaluate and to understand others is, of course, part of the getting-acquainted process.

B. No dating those who display poor taste such as rebellious dress or hairstyle.

C. No attendance or participation in worldly activities such as dances, movies, parked car dates, or petting. Love waits (I Thessalonians 4:5-6; Hebrews 13:4; II Timothy 2:22; I Corinthians 13:4).

D. Parents should be trusted confidants. Where young friends can not always be trusted, mother and dad can. During pre-dating and dating years, the policy of mother and dad should be to lovingly and respectfully seek out and listen to the joys and sorrows of their young person.

E. Dating is an advice and consent process with parents (Romans 13:1; Colossians 3:20).

F. The pace of dating should be such that steady dating will not be a consideration until after high school. The earliest age that even minimal courting will be permitted must be set (e.g., age 16).

Ideas for Dates

Church services	Projects
Church social functions	Bible studies
Athletic events	Topical research projects
Bowling, bicycling, *et cetera*	Dinner fellowships
Family games at home	Cooking at home
Selected plays, concerts	Visiting museums
Clean, wax car	Re-do furniture, *et cetera*
Ministries together	Planning functions

Failure to bring one's child to marriage as a virgin often brings public shame to the child, to the parents, and the father is accountable for this before God (I Samuel 3:13; Proverbs 19:26).

As God's undershepherds, parents have the authority to lovingly superintend their children as a demonstration of God's power for the good, for the family reputation, and to establish the child's development for the future (Colossians 3:20a; Proverbs 29:15).

Chapter Three

Straight Thinking in Analysis

Understanding is a wellspring of life . . .. Proverbs 16:22a
In the beginning was the Word, and the Word was with
God . . .. All things were made by him; and without him
was not any thing made that was made. In him was life;
and the life was the light of men. John 1:1a, 3-4

As was said of Joseph, it pays to be diligent and honest in the development and use of our mind. What an advantage it is to know that decisions based upon emotions can not be trusted, and that by the power of God's indwelling Spirit the counterfeit ways of the world can be foreseen and rejected.

Disagreement with others can be good. Disagreement may bring important matters into focus which are essential for the success and safety of our family, our church, or our career. It is not disagreements but sinful responses to disagreements which are the root problem. The key concern is—what treatment does the Bible advise for handling disagreements?

As a background for straight thinking, it is helpful to review the starkness of values now being advanced by contemporary liberalism.

1. **The elimination of God**: man loses the capacity to make right moral decisions, Romans 1:21, 23, 28.
2. **Doing away with the truth**: presenting the moral value of truth as evil and evil as good, Romans 1:18, 25.
3. **The deification and empowerment of elitists:** dogma for political correctness, Romans 1:23, 28.
4. **The use of feel-good emotions to justify sin**: when nothing can be pronounced as "sin," the people self-destruct wondering, "Why?" They are justifying and prioritizing moral deviancy.
5. **Glorification of death**: suicide, abortion, infanticide, euthanasia, and homosexuality (which imposes two forms of death—absence of procreation and terminal illness). The glorification of death keeps the masses blind to the fact that death is man's enemy and death without Christ ends all hope for salvation from the consequences of their sin.
6. **Theological compromise**: truth does not bend in its governance of events, but compromise in the definition of truth denies the value of truth as man's friend. Those standing for truth are in the center of a truth-hating storm. They do not succumb because they know that God's Word is man's friend.

The First Principle of Life Is the Preservation of Life. Allowing our self-will to have priority over God's Word and empowerment for life is foolish. Emotions such as anger, fear and jealousy are damaging to a person's physical, psychological and spiritual health. This subject is dealt with in chapter 18 of *None of These Diseases*, published by Baker Book Company in the year 2000. Medical doctors S. I. McMillen and David Stern remind us that the vast nerve network of the brain "reaches out to every organ of the body." Electrical and hormonal upsets change "the chemistry of the body and make it sick."

Some people believe that God randomly chose to label certain thoughts and practices as sin, but this is not true. In love, God identified for us those things which are harmful and labeled them sin. "For God sent not his Son into the world to condemn the world; but that the world through him might be saved" (John 3:17). The harmful nature of sin and the life practices which support health and happiness are spelled out for us by God in the Bible. Though sin brings death, sanctification (learning to walk with God) brings life.

All of us experience suffering which has no connection whatsoever to our own sin. Wars, exploitation by others, violent weather, and diseases followed the entry of Satan, recorded in chapter three of Genesis. But God, as Creator of the world, has eternal purposes for man that transcend Satan's evil work and are beyond man's understanding.

As Job found out, ". . . all things work together [ultimately] for good to them that love God, to them who are the called according to his purpose" (Romans 8:28).

Man's capacity to think and make choices is a precious gift, an avenue for fellowshipping with God. Had God forced mankind to obey, their fellowship with Him would not have had the noble character of shared interests that constitutes true fellowship. Man made a wrong choice by rejecting God and this brought grief and pain to the heart of God. "He is despised and rejected of men; a man of sorrows, and acquainted with grief: and we hid as it were our faces from him; he was despised, and we esteemed him not" (Isaiah 53:3).

God spoke to His people saying, ". . . I have no pleasure in the death of the wicked; but that the wicked turn from his way and live: turn ye, turn ye from your evil ways; for why will ye [choose to do those things which cause you to] die, O house of Israel?" (Ezekiel 33:11).

When Adam and Eve chose to reject God's leadership, mankind became spiritually insensitive and vulnerable to the deception of Satan, who is the father of lies and of death. But,

"For God so loved the world [you and me], that he gave his only begotten Son [to die on the cross in atonement for man's sin], that whosoever believeth in him [accepts Christ] should not perish, but have everlasting life [is born-again spiritually and has fellowship with the God of heaven]" (John 3:16).

The Greek word in the Bible for "save" and "salvation" is *sozo*, which can also be translated "to make whole." Christ came not only to save but also to heal believers from emotional pain and spiritual dysfunction caused by their sin. "Who his own self bare our sins in his own body on the tree, that we, being dead to sins [empowered to identify and reject sin], should live unto righteousness: by whose stripes ye were healed" (I Peter 2:24).

Truth does not bend. Straight thinking and lasting success call for honesty with self and with God. Justification (sins forgiven) comes by faith in Christ. Insensibility to the damning nature of sin is lethal to the soul. The beliefs that we adopt determine whether we belong to God or to the world, thereby determining both our earthly and eternal destiny.

A young man who is suffering the consequences of sin during his final weeks of life needs little imagination to perceive the discomfort of hell. Hell is real. Living a good life, that is, treating people kindly and hurting only a few by "little sins," does not even begin to deal with the question of the injustice of those sins, let alone satisfy or compensate for the harm caused. ". . . Blessed are they whose iniquities are forgiven, and whose sins are covered" (Romans 4:7). "For whosoever shall call upon the name of the Lord shall be saved [from the price that injustice and sin extract from life]" (Romans 10:13).

Understanding is the wellspring of life. The value of the understanding received when one invites Christ in as the Lord over their decisions for life is priceless. The BC/AD partition on the calendar reflects the enormous influence Christ's redemptive gift has made on history. "Nineteen wide centuries have come and gone and today He is the centerpiece of the human race and the leader of the column of progress. I am far within the mark when I say that all the armies that ever marched and all the navies that ever were built, and all of the parliaments that ever have sat, and all the kings that ever reigned put together have not affected the life of man upon this earth as powerfully as has that one solitary life, Jesus of Nazareth." *One Solitary Life,* adapted from a sermon by James Allen Frances and published by Judson Press in 1926 (see emotionsanddecisions.com).

Have you invited Christ into your life? "But for us also, to whom it shall be imputed, if we believe on him that raised up Jesus our Lord from the dead; Who was delivered for our offences, and was raised again for our justification. Therefore being justified by faith, we have peace with God through our Lord Jesus Christ" (Romans 4:24-25; 5:1).

"Wherefore the law [unchanging and just rules for treating self and others] was our schoolmaster to bring us unto Christ, that we might be justified [have our sins forgiven] by faith [in Christ's provision]. But after that faith is come, we are no longer under a schoolmaster. For ye are all the children of God by faith in Christ Jesus" (Galatians 3:24-26). "Therefore if any man be in Christ, he is a new creature: old things are passed away; behold, all things are become new" (II Corinthians 5:17).

For you have been ". . . born again, not of corruptible seed, but of incorruptible, by the word of God, which liveth and abideth for ever."
I Peter 1:23

We determine and choose the end result by the faith we choose at the beginning! Those who start with the elimination of God end up with death! To fix the brokenness and stop the emotional pain, we must turn our eyes back to God's way, the only beginning that brings life!

STEPS TO HAPPINESS & PEACE WITH GOD
(The key is with whom you choose to place your faith)

1. **RECOGNIZE GOD'S PLAN - HAPPINESS IN LIFE**
   God loves you and has a wonderful plan for your life.
   The BIBLE says: "For God so loved
   the world, that he gave his only begotten Son,
   that whosoever believeth in him should not
   perish, but have everlasting life" (John 3:16).

2. **REALIZE MAN'S PROBLEM - SEPARATION**
   People choose to disobey God their Creator
   and, thusly separated, go astray.
   The BIBLE says: "For all have sinned, and
   come short of the glory of God" (Romans 3:23).

3. **RESPOND TO GOD'S REMEDY - CHRIST'S SACRIFICE**
   God's love bridges the gap of separation between
   God and you. When Jesus Christ died on the
   cross and rose from the grave, He paid the
   penalty for your sins. "But God commendeth
   his love toward us, in that, while we were yet
   sinners, Christ died for us" (Romans 5:8).

4. **RECEIVE CHRIST**
   You cross the bridge into God's family when
   you ask Christ to come into your life.
   The BIBLE says: "But as many as received
   him, to them gave he power to become
   the sons of God . . ." (John 1:12).

Receiving Christ involves four things: admitting your spiritual need, the desire to turn from your sin, believing that Jesus Christ died for you on the cross, and receiving Jesus into your heart and life.

The BIBLE says (Christ is speaking): "Behold, I stand at the door, and knock: if any man hear my voice, and open the door, I will come in to him, and will sup with him, and he with me" (Revelation 3:20); and, "For whosoever shall call upon the name of the Lord shall be saved" (Romans 10:13).

A sample of the BELIEVER'S PRAYER:
"Dear Lord Jesus, I know I am an unworthy sinner and I believe You died on the cross for my sins. Please forgive me of my sins and transform me into a new person. I surrender control of my life to you today. Thank You for saving me and giving me life eternal. Amen."

Biblical outline adopted in part from *The God of All Comfort* by Hannah W. Smith, and published by Moody Press.

The old nature does get the upper hand on occasion in the life of a Christian, but fellowship with God, wisdom, and insight needed for reliable decisions are restored when he repents. "If we confess our sins, he is faithful and just to forgive us our sins, and to cleanse us from all unrighteousness" (I John 1:9).

Those who trust God have every reason to be optimistic. "Now we have received, not the spirit of the world, but the spirit which is of God; that we might know the things [hidden to the natural man] that are freely given to us of God" (I Corinthians 2:12).

"Now unto him that is able to keep you from falling, and to present you faultless before the presence of his glory [in heaven] with exceeding joy" (Jude 24).

Chapter Four

The Citizens' Report

It was my privilege to chair a Grand Jury for the 11th Judicial District of Iowa which investigated university activities and made several recommendations for changes in higher education. The jury's chief concern was the educational environment and its impact upon the emotions and decision-making ability of students.

Though the jury study covered the 1960s, it is very relevant to an understanding of the chapter which follows, entitled "Public Education Now." The same emotionally charged deception that was occurring in our universities is now occurring at the lower level elementary and secondary schools. Leftist anti-American, anti-family, and sex education which borders upon pornography are commonplace. **It is important at this point to note that most professors and public school teachers are well-intended citizens and doing their best. They have no more control over the curriculum for the above subjects than do parents**.

Seven citizens were chosen at random for the jury duty. Upon the recommendation of the Story County attorney, Charles Vanderbur, the judge asked me to be the foreman. The judge, impaneled at the time said (paraphrased), "Mr. Norris, this jury is the most powerful agency of government, and the jurors have the authority to investigate any operation of government within Story County that they deem appropriate."

We had certain fixed duties and were guided through them by the county attorney. Our first duty was to inspect the Story County Home. The staff provided us with a sumptuous meal. I gave the county attorney the opportunity to lead in thanksgiving for the meal and was glad to respond when he asked me to say the prayer.

The judge's statement that the jury had authority to investigate any operation of government in Story County stayed with me. News reports suggested that drugs, immorality, and disrespect for constitutional authority had become an acceptable academic menu in our universities. With about six months left in our term, I suggested to the county attorney that the jury should investigate what was going on at Iowa State University. He said, "Dave, I'll do anything I can to help you." He provided us with tape recordings of campus presentations and clerical assistance as needed. After hearing the first tape, the jury members gave the go-ahead to undertake an investigation.

God's providence was evident throughout this experience. My challenge as the foreman was to get unanimous agreement for significant recommendations from four Republican and three Democrat jurors. The jury moved resolutely. Though the impact upon the problems is now marginal, several legislative directives for changes in the administration of Iowa colleges and universities resulted. The greatest impact was that the halo over higher education was removed, and it ceased to be politically untouchable. The presentment received nationwide attention. Requests for copies of the jury's presentment came from leaders in the administrations of both California Governor Ronald Reagan and President Richard Nixon.

The university's power to shape public opinion was and remains immense. It had a TV station and a prestigious media network. It had political, religious, and social studies courses, statewide extension offices, and adult education outreach. It did everything it could to discredit the Grand Jury's work. Initially, however, news of the presentment was unimpeded. The university president and all members of the Iowa Board of Regents except one were out of the state. I was later told that a university administrative vice-president was briefing the incoming extension course attendees and denigrating the work of the jury. Eventually, a county extension officer attending one of the on-campus short courses stood up and strongly criticized the vice-president's presentation, and with that the practice was discontinued.

Except for the *Des Moines Register* and radical student publications, most news reports were accurate. Those who were critical were very spirited in their objections. A *Des Moines Register* headline read, "ISU President Lashes Out at 'Distorted' Report by Jury." Later, the Iowa State University Press published a book about the Iowa Civil Liberties Union entitled, *Freedom in Iowa.* This publication showered ISU President Parks with honors and attacked the work and reputation of several Iowa leaders past and present, including myself.

The presentment was well documented. One news article reported that the Iowa Civil Liberties Union had decided they would not sue the Grand Jury. Another paper reported that an on-going effort had failed to get the new judge, Harvey Uhlenhopp, serving the 11th Judicial District, to dismiss the presentment. Within two years Judge Uhlenhopp was elevated to the Iowa Supreme Court.

With the assistance of the editor of the local newspaper, Rod Riggs, the presentment was given to Harrison Webber who headed the central news office in Des Moines, Iowa. As agreed, Mr. Webber released a summary of the presentment after I was assured that Judge Uhlenhopp had received the presentment.

This writing is the only report of the procedure followed

by the jury. I was concerned that some reporters and editors would twist what was said. Consequently, reporters were told that I would respond to inquiries in writing, and this brought their interest to a halt. I personally received approximately 100 letters from citizens, all of whom appreciated the jury's work.

Arrangements were made for a local firm to print and handle requests for the presentment. Later, I received a call from them informing me that the university had purchased all the remaining copies, so I instructed them to print 500 more.

The Grand Jury members all contributed to the report. From a leadership perspective, I did my best to see that they were fully informed. There was a considerable amount of material to review. A few campus administrators and faculty members met with us to give their perspective. Following each meeting, I wrote a brief of what seemed relevant and presented it to the jury members at the next meeting. They would approve most of the brief, and that became our presentment.

Portions of the Grand Jury Presentment follow, word-for-word, with additions for clarification in parentheses. Commentary about jury findings is below the line at the bottom of the page.

POWER TO CAPTURE A NATION THROUGH INDOCTRINATION OF ITS YOUTH

For many years, psychologists and educators have recognized the processes by which thought and behavioral patterns acquired in youth become the basis for adult motivation. In modern times, thoughtful observers have become progressively aware that moral, social and political concepts implanted during the time of mental immaturity not only participate in the conduct of later in life, but, once acquired, such concepts become dominant and often unalterable in the adult. **Thus, captive audiences of immature minds provide powerful and much prized forums for anti-Judeo-Christian, anti-American indoctrination.**

Educational environments (for the soft sciences), left unguarded (by citizen and legislative action), can easily be captured by alien militants and, in due course, transformed into climates of unquestioning (one-sided leftist) social and political opinion.

Dr. I. L. Kandell, a refugee from Romania and professor at Columbia University, aptly lamented (education devoid of established knowledge), ". . . is the most Communist feature of the Communist Revolution and the most Nazi expression of the National Socialist Revolution." Knowledge is not always wisdom.

The modern term for atheistic humanist-based worldview is "political correctness." Opposing points of view, namely the moral, religious liberty, and political principles upon which America has prospered, are censored from the classroom. Consequently, many young minds are turned away from the basic foundation upon which responsible liberty depends. The non-sectarian theistic alternative leads to the conclusion that our liberties come from God, not government or some religio/social/politically correct elite. It is the higher authority concept for law that placed America far and above the other nations. This principle, adopted from the Hebrew-Christian Bible, provides cover for liberty of conscience by protecting the rights of all the moral religions to practice and compete publicly with other beliefs, Christian and non-Christian. If as a reader there is any confusion about this history, I recommend the reading of Chapter Six, *American Principles,* before proceeding with this and the next chapter.

Many radical leaders are college and university graduates. Fidel Castro, who took control of Cuba, has a Juris Doctorate degree.

THE AMERICAN IDEAL REFLECTED IN THE *CONSTITUTIONS* OF THE STATES

1. "We, the People of the State of Iowa, grateful to the Supreme Being for the blessings hitherto enjoyed, and feeling our dependence on Him for a continuation of those blessings, do ordain and establish a free and independent government, by the name of the STATE OF IOWA."

2. "Government is instituted (by the people) for the protection, security and benefit of the people."

3. *Bill of Rights.* Section 1: "All men are, by nature, free and equal, and have certain inalienable rights—among which are those of enjoying and defending life and liberty, acquiring, possessing and protecting property, and pursuing and obtaining safety and happiness."

4. Section 2: "All political power is inherent in the people" (the clique who are supposed to run things).

5. ". . . they (the people) have the right at all times, to alter or reform the government, whenever the public good may require it" (provision for peaceful revolution).

Secular militants who oppose our form of government are not new. Control over the use of taxpayer funds and government power has always been a test of wills. The Judeo-Christian approach to reality for government foundations was vehemently opposed during the writing of the *Iowa Constitution.*

6. (Provision for a frequent unrestricted exchange of ideas for education and government policy, no matter how radical. The candidates for office are judged and chosen by mature citizens at the ballot box.)

7. Article IX, *Iowa Constitution*, 2nd School . . . Section 3: **"The General Assembly shall encourage by all suitable means the intellectual, scientific, MORAL and agricultural improvement."**

OBSERVATIONS IN THE PROBLEM AREA

(The Iowa State University Press published a book for the Iowa Civil Liberties Union, *Freedom in Iowa*, following publication of the Grand Jury Presentment. Among many false statements in the book was the statement on page 47 that the Grand Jury "never defined" the word *radicals*.)

At this point perhaps we (the jury) should define to some extent what we mean in this report by "radicals" and "militants" in the context of their behavior on campus (and) as expressed in our interviews and investigation.

I. Their number one goal, both stated and apparent, is that they desire to control the useful university apparatus for a base to promote (their ideology) and direct their activities. There is no apparent limit; university news media (college for training and licensing primary and secondary teachers), selection of guest speakers, extension outlets, *et cetera*.

An example of the power of radicals at ISU (Iowa State University), called to our attention, was provided by a citizen who had contacted a department head. He suggested that the coming News Editors' Seminar might be informed by the University of an Official Pamphlet about the techniques of Communist propaganda in the news media. The citizen was told that it was not the business of the university to get involved in politics. The citizen was shocked to later read in the newspaper that an associate professor of history had lectured the editors on the possible future problem with certain local political groups. (This university outreach was clearly a program for undermining the rights and credibility of citizens who oppose leftist policy.)

II. They have a general goal of destroying and tearing down. (Hateful talk leads to hateful acts, and immoral advocacy leads to immoral acts.) Radical salesmen appeal to idealistic students with words calculated to destroy their youthful faith in their heritage. The following (provided by the County Attorney to the jury) are quotations from one of many paid speakers at ISU: 'I spend about 90% of my time now on college campuses. This is the most morally polluted, insane nation on the face of this earth and it is your job to change it.' 'And I say to you youngsters in the process of trying to make this peacefully orderly transition of bringing up the constitution over the capitalists, if they offer you too much resistance, then destroy them.' '. . . let me tell you something, black folks used them two words, _____ _____. We used it a lot but we didn't invent it. White folks invented those two words, you just called it Oedipus Rex and dirty enough to teach world literature with it.' '. . . Let's always remember that flag still ain't nothing but a rag, like all of the other flags on the face of this earth . . ..'

This was not an isolated example but typical of much of the educational approach we observed.

In place of established knowledge, they (contemporary liberals) want relativism as the accepted (approach to education). Relativism for purposes of this discussion refers to the denial of absolutes and puts evil on a par with discerned truth as a legitimate teaching subject.

In the area of society and human nature, such denial, when implemented, detaches future generations from past experience. Oddly enough, that is the very reason taxpayers fund colleges and universities. Tolerating such foolishness gives a teaching license to those who promote illicit sex, the use of decimating drugs, flag burning, *et cetera.* and places in question historically known good.

Such a position on fundamental tenets raises a very interesting question. If the desirability of sexual virtue and undesirability of overnight co-habitation in single student dorms is as they say a matter of opinion, if in fact sexual virtue and many other tenets such as basic honesty are not established knowledge suitable for classroom doctrine—what is the good of having humanities courses at all? When a radical teacher lectures, what is he accomplishing with taxpayers' money?

III. Tactics used by radicals disregard the minimum teacher standard of honesty. It is not unusual to hear them proclaim the virtues of equality and love, and extol violence, hatred, and the use of harmful drugs in the same speech. In their effort to present a one-sided picture they suppress opposing views. One jury interviewee (a professor) stated his concern—if students hear a lie often enough some believe it!

IV. Tactics are aggressive, domineering and, when needed, ruthless in character. In such cases the person with average courtesy is no match. The most aggressive prevail over those teachers who feel obligated to spend their time teaching and learning rather than contending with and being buffeted by verbal terrorism. One of their tactics is rule by committee domination. They pressure administrators to relinquish their duty in a specific area and turn it over to a committee (see the last page of this chapter.

These practices by employees all fall below what the taxpaying public, in our opinion, expect and have a right to expect of the teachers they hire.

SUMMARY FROM GRAND JURY FINDINGS

The concrete evidence of failures . . . is well illustrated by the article entitled 'New Left's Boasts: We are organizing sedition.' According to the article, the *New York Times* asked an Iowa State University student '. . . where he picked up his radical ideas.' The article referred to a teacher by name and concluded, 'He was a history teacher here (Iowa State University) two years ago. I took a course in *Ideas of Western Civilization* from him. That got me started.' There . . . (is no) doubt that some teachers are guilty of using their status to effectively subvert or undermine the morals and allegiance of some students.

Tolerance for the breakdown in the citizen authority chain of command, set in place to control the education, makes retention of citizen taxpayer values impossible. This parallels the tyranny of medieval kings who in partnership with government and at the expense of the people controlled education.

The atheistic humanist approach to governance of education is illustrated by a more recent event at ISU. Through denigrating talk and dishonest portrayal of academic freedom, a few tenured professors forced the discontinuation of a very popular university course dealing with the science that is allied to creation. The course came too close to violating the secular humanist presupposition upon which their theory of evolution, anti-American traditions, and anti-morality are constructed. This occurred in spite of the fact that the course was taught by a respected and highly ranked professor/administrator at Iowa State University.

Our investigation indicates that the main reason for the youthful rebellion and attitude of carelessness in their morals is the loss of confidence of the young in the wisdom embedded in their heritage. Failure to clearly implant these truths detaches future generations from past experience, the very basis of education (curriculum orientation).

In the field of morality all basic truths have been apprehended. All the changing conditions we hear so much about do not affect the validity or applicability of the central directives of human conduct. These truths are demonstrable in terms of benefits and as to how it is that those who disregard them fall easily into alien pitfalls of Fascism, lawlessness, drug addiction, *et cetera*. **There is no greater contribution a teaching institution can make to human progress and purpose than to endow students at all levels with this knowledge. All other aspects of education ought to be subservient.**

Those who place their present faith and future hope in law enforcement to conduct humanity to brighter times ignore . . ., a fundamental psychological truth. Legal and material attempts to correct human conduct resulting from improper training must all end in failure. It is impossible to superimpose an effective code of ethics through compulsion. Police force provides nothing more corrective than temporary control of faulty behavior that is traceable to education's failure to implant established knowledge of morality and the precepts of individual responsibility into the educated.

It is teacher employment guarantees in our laws that are working against the public interest by empowering teachers who impose an anti-morality, anti-democracy agenda.

WHERE TO GO FOR THE SOLUTION

The frustrating inability of the public to correct the distortion of academic freedom is due, in the Grand Jury's view, to the failure of the people to see the continuation of the atrocious abuses by radicals as a breakdown in the responsibility-authority-control principle that it really is. Any organization, educational or otherwise, is an attempt at cooperation. Cooperation is not possible unless responsibility and authority go hand-in-hand.

The parents and taxpayers delegated their responsibility-authority powers indirectly through a chain-of-command selection of people who want to teach and (honestly) **agree with public policy.**

The system of organization varies in the several states, but in Iowa the Board of Regents (chosen by the Governor) is responsible to the public for education at the state universities. It is at this level, the Board of Regents who must lay down corrective policy on behalf of the people. If the problem is ever corrected . . . (changes must be imposed by the public), at this level.

The taxpayers, having the final responsibility for the universities, quite properly should have the authority to change the Board of Regents' membership or take other measures if they find themselves in disagreement with Board policy. If the established procedures for governing at this level leave the Regents insensitive to public interest then it is time to update governing procedures.

Discretion in exercising authority, regardless of where it is vested, is assured. The citizen public, having given the Board of Regents (in this case), the responsibility to implement public policy, must leave them the authority to go to the university president, who has the executive responsibility of the university. The university president, vested with the responsibility by the Board of Regents, has the authority to change his aides if he believes they are not carrying out his ideas (in the public interest), *et cetera* on down the line.

MOST IMPORTANT EDUCATIONAL CHANGE NEEDED

1. Regents' policy changes which will sufficiently define and implement the elimination of moral pollution by faculty and paid speakers will by all suitable means encourage "moral . . . improvement," [*Constitution of the State of Iowa, Article IX, 2nd School . . . Sec. 3*].

2. There is a need for increased emphasis on the American ideal at all levels of education (respect for our Republic 'grateful to the Supreme Being for the blessings hitherto enjoyed' as stated in the *Iowa Constitution*). We believe this ideal needs (to be a continuing emphasis) from kindergarten through to maturity. Our revolutionary concepts are a most exciting and important subject. Our soldier boys have been dying for this ideal. Education, as never before, should clearly teach it. Even in imperfection it has achieved greatness for America unparalleled in history. Every individual is important, and the mature public makes the decisions over government. Something alien (atheist humanist) based governments do not provide.

It seems rather clear that the nerve center for society, the power for social revolution, is inherent in the adult electorate rather than in the schools and that the radical missionaries should be sent to the electorate, not to the captive audience of youthful minds.

The idea . . . that the people of this land should not be trusted with the complexities of education is absurd. The very definition of practical greatness, which built America, entrusts the educational and political emphasis to the control of the people. This is much safer than providing a haven (employment guarantees) for . . . teachers (in the soft sciences) who refuse to be responsible to the public and emphasize what they want with impunity.

Out in Iowa

From the Boston Record, edition of Jan. 7, 1969:

"They don't kid around out in Iowa. A grand jury there wants 'moral pollution by faculty and paid speakers' at Iowa State University discouraged by changes in the humanities curriculum. The grand jury charged that 'the militant radical activist, both teacher and-student, is involved in the humanities,' and called on the State Board of Regents to make 'corrective' policy changes.

"The jury began the investigation after reports of 'student radicals and other activists using campus media to pulpiteer, sensationalize and otherwise promote illicit sex, drug use, draft evasion, and defamation of our country.'

"The jury's report said 'there is a need for increased emphasis at all levels of education of the American ideal. Our soldiers have been dying for this ideal. Education as never before should clearly teach it.' So say we."

Ames Daily Tribune
Tues., Jan. 14, 1969

RIGHT OF TAXPAYERS TO CONTROL EDUCATION CHALLENGED

Who has academic freedom, the parent/taxpayer or the teacher? Is the parent, who once had academic freedom, now to be deprived because a teacher was hired? Most agree that anyone can teach what he pleases on his own responsibility, but must not yield to his cry of academic freedom and rob taxpayers of their freedom to direct public education in the public's interest, based upon the learning process and established knowledge.

GRAND JURY REPORT

Moral Faults at Iowa State Hit

By **CELIENE NOLD BRUCE**

AMES, Iowa—(AP)—A grand jury in Story County, Iowa, wants "moral pollution by faculty and paid "speakers" at Iowa State University discouraged by changes in the humanities curriculum.

"The militant, radical activist, both teacher and student, is involved in the humanities," said the jury after a three-month investigation.

UP TO BOARD

The jury said it was up to the State Board of Regents to make "corrective" policy changes, and said regents' membership should be changed if the public isn't satisfied with what it does.

"There is a need for increased emphasis at all levels of education of the American ideal," the jury report said. "Our soldier boys have been dying for this ideal. Education as never before should clearly teach it."

The jury said it began the investigation after frequent reports of "student radicals and other activists using campus media to pulpiteer, sensational-

DENVER POST
12/29/68

ize and otherwise promote illicit sex, drug use, draft evasion, and defamation of our country."

ISU, around state u the nin

"Is i the Bo definiti sibility discont liars, v our he ples or ic free

The that ha the hu lem "ı admini "level

The who tr "faith nothin; their o

"Our by the about :

are in
much
have .
jority
world,
"Wh
tures,
with 1
What
ward
moral ı

January 21, 1969 *Page 1*

LETTERS to the EDITOR

January 15, 1969

Editor, The Journal:

As one of the tens of thousands who admire the action of your Grand Jury, I wish to commend Foreman Norris and his jury for their courageous and true Americanism, in focusing Public attention on the perverted minority anarchists who would destroy what we have left in American, and deliver us unto our enemies.

As one who has always been proud of ISU, let me express my shame for its leaders who were not wise enough to remain quiet — evidence of the apparent determination of High Education to continue its sucidial plunge of self destruction. And believe me, few of your readers have spent more time or money on Education than I.

Patriotic Americans are demanding that funds to these perverted elements be CUT OFF! This is the one language the anarchists and their teachers understand.

Very truly yours,
E. Allen
Box 502
Burlington, N.D.

Nevada Journal Tuesday

PROBLEMS FEED BACK AND COMPOUND IF NOT CORRECTED

No single level of education can be considered in a vacuum, good or bad. But it is going on! The students of colleges are, after all, the graduates of American elementary and secondary schools. We, the adults and teachers of today, are the graduates of high schools, colleges, and universities in the recent past. Not only are various levels of American education interrelated, but the problems also feed back upon one another to produce a complex of relationships which affect us all and must be handled wisely. In professions such as medicine or architecture, failures soon become apparent and are corrected. A faulty experiment impacting the social-political mindset may not be detected for two or three generations, when it is too late to reverse and avoid disaster.

End of Presentment

Hostility against the traditional American approach to education is an attack on the heart of America. When citizen control of taxpayer-funded education is superceded by non-representative powers, tyranny is bound to follow, and tyranny against the moral fiber of our youth and nation we now have.

At the time of the Grand Jury study we did not realize the linkage between the American Association of University Professors (AAUP) and, what appears to be a prosecutory arm, the leftist American Civil Liberties Union (ACLU) lawyers. Teacher employee contracts structured according to their academic freedom and tenure definitions shift the decision-making authority from the president of the university to the militant liberal faculty. In reality, it is the aggressive professors/teachers, not the president or superintendent (hired as the administer for taxpayer-funded education), who are the administrators. The president is very busy putting out fires, lobbying reporters, alumni, and the legislature for more money (see pages 74 -78).

Also, the ACLU/AAUP **version of academic freedom is not a legal concept.** It is wholly dependent upon the internal culture of the faculty at the universities and the lower level government (public) schools. In other words, there is no mechanism which the taxpaying public can implement to assure that both the theistic and the atheist perspectives for soft science instruction will be taught truthfully. The tradition for education in America requires a truthful presentation of both worldviews based upon outcomes they have generated in human history (see pages 110-111). The control mechanism for this is a firm linkage between an independent local citizen school board and school administrator. The larger the school, the weaker the linkage. Education was undermined by school consolidation, pushed under the guise of cost savings. What happened was a decline in learning and a phenomenal increase in costs. Going along with that big mistake came the corrupting influence of collective paternalism. To this day, the moral foundations of home-taught students and students from smaller schools tend to be strengthened rather than be ridiculed and undermined. The students also get better grades. **In contrast, atheistic-based instruction which flows from monopoly secularism trashes belief in God and moral values**.

Your voice on behalf of sanity in education is the key. By insisting that soft science instruction be **delivered by non-government citizen choice entities,** leftist educators' undermining belief in constitutional intent and turning government power against moral law would run into hard times. When teacher unions no longer operate as extensions of government, education will again benefit from the pressure of competition, and the taxpaying public will again be treated with respect. The many thousands of honest and morally upright teachers will also be treated respectfully.

Chapter Five

Public Education Now

STATUS AND BEGINNINGS

Education Reform and Failure—The public education system in our nation is abounding with problems. Virtually everyone acknowledges this fact. Reforms promoted by academia turn out to be repackaged and renamed failures.

According to a November 2001 progress survey by the National Assessment of Education, fewer than 40 percent of 21 to 25-year-olds were able to interpret an article by a newspaper columnist. In less than forty years, Scholastic Aptitude Test (SAT) scores have declined to the point that the United States now ranks 14th in science and 18th in math, which is far below many of the world's industrialized nations.

College seniors have no better grasp of "general cultural knowledge" than did the high school graduates in the 1950s. The average correct responses for modern college seniors on a series of questions was 53.5 percent compared to 54.5 percent of high school graduates in 1955. This is from a survey by Zogby International done in April 2002 for the Princeton, New Jersey based National Association of Scholars and addressed by NAS President Stephen H. Balch in December 2002.

In addition to diminished academic learning, social and moral deviancy introduced by public schools increases in our communities and adds to the prison population.

Since September 11, 2001, the public understands that we are at war with Islamic radicals, but few have a clue that America is being attacked in a more harmful way from within through its public schools by militants of the secular left. Both of these groups desire to alter our thinking and control our lives.

The National Commission on Excellence in Education issued a non-partisan report in 1983 which is still considered the premier overview of public education in America. The report stated that the decline in our public education system might well be "viewed as an act of war" by an "unfriendly foreign power." "Our concern," the Commission reported, "goes well beyond matters such as industry and commerce. It also includes the intellectual, moral, and spiritual strengths of our people which knit together the very fabric of our society" (*A Nation at Risk,* United States Government Printing Office, Washington, D.C.).

Some people do see what is happening. "The percentage of public school teachers nationwide who are choosing to protect their own children by sending them to private schools is over twice the rate of non-teacher parents" (*World,* August 5, 1995). "More than half of parents with children in public schools . . . would send their children to private schools if they could afford to . . ." (The *Daily Tribune,* Ames, Iowa, October 11, 1995).

The problem is not that students are not being taught. They are being taught plenty. In addition to large increases in spending locally, federal spending for elementary and secondary education has gone from 7 billion in 1985 to 22.5 billion in 2000 and just 32% of the fourth graders read proficiently (U.S. Department of Education Web Page, January 2003).

THE NATURE OF THE PROBLEM

How did it get so bad? With a stream of reforms, why are

things worse instead of better? The deterioration is the natural result of a change from a Judeo-Christian view of reality to a godless humanistic worldview governing curriculum content. As public education grew, a militant and often belligerent breed of progressivist "social engineers" pushed their way into leadership circles. This group included Professor John Dewey, acknowledged by educators to be the father of modern day public education.

HISTORY PRECEEDING THE YOUTHFUL RADICALISM OF THE 1960s

Many of the men who helped lift humanity out of the deprivation of the Dark Ages were known as humanists. This power for a Renaissance and a Reformation was found in the return of the Bible to the people. The founders of modern science, including Leonardo da Vinci, Johannes Kepler, Francis Bacon, Blaise Pascal, Nicolaus Copernicus, Isaac Newton, Louis Pasteur, and George Washington Carver, were all men of God and the Bible. Deceptively, those now advocating the other worldview which is **a militant faith in and determination to impose a godless ideological belief upon humanity call themselves** *humanists*.

Outspoken humanists such as John Dewey, Bertrand Russell, and Julian Huxley were published atheists. Belief about man's beginnings, meaning, and purpose, held by the secular humanists and Marxists, is found in the ancient philosophy of evolution. Charles Darwin (1809-1882) advanced this godless philosophy of origins (which has since been revised many times), but he claimed it to be "science."

Conscious of public rejection, atheist professors began to call themselves "Progressivists" and "Secular Humanists." The religious *Humanist Manifesto I*, adopted in 1933, and the *Humanist Manifesto II* (1973) are atheistic. In the 1930s, humanists redoubled their attacks against American education philosophy in teacher training, journalism, history, and the law schools.

The Progressivists began by assuming [arguing ve-
hemently] that the older education had been a general
failure. They told the world that earlier teachers were
a breed of ill-equipped, overly bookish tyrants. Hence
they argued for progressive teachers' colleges, life-
adjustment programs and a child-centered
[juvenile rights] classroom (Neil McClukey, *America*,
December 1, 1956).

Not only must school teachers and principals be
exemplars of openmindedness and free inquiry, but
severally and collectively, they must be prepared to
proclaim their FAITH in that OPENMINDEDNESS
AND FREE INQUIRY.' Here we must hearken to
Dewey: '[T]he administrator will . . . realize that
public education is essentially education of the public:
directly, through teachers and students . . . **in the
transformation of society**' (Robert Hoffman, *A Note
on Academic Freedom, Schoolmen Must Declare Their
Faith, Phi Delta Kappan*, 44:185-188, January,
1963—cited in *Foundations of American Education*,
Allyn & Bacon, Inc., 1970, p. 192).

Many teacher-training colleges, the National Education Association, and their affiliates were co-opted by militant
secular progressivists. They eventually recast taxpayer-
funded universities and lower level public schools as un-
ionized government bureaucracies, and the traditional
American view of reality was pushed aside.

Significant members of the team working against the educational transfer of basic knowledge or beliefs upon which
responsible liberty depend appear to be the American Civil
Liberties Union, its state affiliates, and the American Association of University Professors. Well-paid professors appear
to be providing much of the strategies, communication, and
funding needed for ACLU lawyers.

The imposition of the secular (atheistic) view of reality on the minds of law students explains the ignominy of a Supreme Court majority that would make prayer in public schools unlawful and overthrow the abortion laws of all the 50 states. Prior to the tyranny of these rulings, public education had the protection of the people who choose like-minded representatives to carry out their will in education matters. Prior to the arbitrary decision of the liberal majority on the court, millions of highly pain-sensitive individuals had the protection of the abortion laws according to the will of the citizens in the 50 states.

The following reflects the tyranny inherent in the mind-altering doctrine of secular humanism and its liberal cousins.

1. **The elimination of God**: man loses the capacity to make right moral decisions (Romans 1:21, 23, 28).
1. **Doing away with the truth**: presenting the moral value of truth as evil and evil as good (Romans 1:18, 25).
2. **The deification and empowerment of elitists**: dogma for political correctness (Romans 1:23, 28).
3. **Feel-good emotions are used to justify sin**: when nothing can be pronounced as "sin," the people self-destruct and wonder why. Contemporary liberals are minimizing and justifying moral deviancy.
4. **Glorification of death**: suicide, abortion, infanticide, euthanasia, and homosexuality (which imposes two forms of death—no conception and a communicable virus which causes death). The glorification of death keeps the masses blind to the fact that death is their enemy, and that death without Christ ends all hope for salvation from the consequences of sin.
6. **Theological compromise**: truth does not bend in its governance of events, but compromise in the definition of truth denies the value of truth as man's friend. Those standing for truth are in the center of a truth-hating storm. They do not succumb because they know that God's Word is man's friend.

We determine and choose the end result by the faith we choose at the beginning. Those who start with the elimination of God end up with death.

Though seductively hidden in education reforms, the flood of godless humanism in school textbooks is freely admitted by humanists in their own publications. The following quote is from the January/February 1976 issue of *The Humanist*:

> Something wonderful, free, unheralded, and of significance to all humanists is happening in the secondary schools. It is the adolescent literature movement. They may burn *Slaughterhouse Five* in North Dakota and ban a number of innocuous books in Kanawah County, but . . . the crazies don't do all that much reading. If they did, they'd find that they have already been defeated. Adolescent literature has opened Pandora's box.

According to secular militants, their goals justify any means. Social progress must not be entrusted to the values of the people. Parallel to the Divine Right of King's doctrine that plagued mankind in the Dark Ages, their goal (social progress) is based upon truth, and only academians know the truth. **This justifies the MEANS which is teacher "tenure guarantees" that give teachers independence from any meaningful parent/taxpayer citizen supervision. Secure in their work, the bishops of progressive education are forcing their version of truth upon American youth which includes their doctrine of OPEN-MINDEDNESS as the justification for their versions of children's rights, values clarification, and multiculturalism. Consequently, the moral backbone of education which gives young people discernment for putting the brakes on their emotions and self-ruin has been stripped from public education.**

Why is it that the public is not generally aware of terribly harmful instruction going on in our own local schools? First, the many good teachers and administrators cannot handle the onslaught of verbal terrorism by tenured leftists which accompanies any objections to their agenda. Many good teachers who can get along without the income just quit in order to separate themselves from the problems. Occasionally, an irate parent will write an editorial in the local newspaper that exposes an incident. Less often, an event which is damaging to the students' minds does get into news copy. Even business people hoping for community growth prefer that prospective newcomer families do not know of the moral and ideological radicalism in the local public school. Though this is only the tip of the iceberg, it is all that the public will probably ever know about harmful moral and ideological instruction in the local schools. The ability of people to identify pornography is rejected by liberal judges, so disgusted parents are turned away from the legal system for a remedy.

We are told that for teacher violations which are not clearly of a non-teaching type of crime, the most that can be done is to reprimand an errant teacher. Teacher union contracts prohibit this reprimand from being included on the teacher's record when he or she moves to another community to teach. An example of atheist humanist mindset follows:

> Parents, nurses, and teachers are the natural enemies of the child because they are the destroyers of freedom. They represent authority from the beginning (Ethel Manin, quoted in *Common Sense and the Child*, 1931).

Graduates of teacher training colleges controlled by secular humanists are themselves the victims of atheist humanist indoctrination. The impact of this ideology upon the minds of students (if believed) produces a determination to oppose traditional American values as they themselves become licensed to teach.

Following the September 11, 2001 bombing of the World Trade Center and Pentagon, one television news report covering the event included an interview of high school students. The students were from what was said to be one of the best New York City public schools. The students interviewed were clearly bewildered by the sudden need to re-evaluate Their anti-American, anti-moral-authority, anti-police perceptions. This student exposure to reality is perhaps one of the very few good things to come out of those diabolical and cruel attacks.

WHAT IS WRONG WITH THE PUBLIC SCHOOLS?

A. PUBLIC SCHOOLS HAVE A LEFTIST POLITICAL BIAS AGAINST AMERICAN HISTORY

As is well known, an understanding of history is important because it is the most reliable basis for evaluating situations and making reliable decisions. How is the distorted view of history being taught in public schools revealed? Instead of teaching the truth they teach a leftist, "revisionist" (anti-family, anti-morality, anti-American-business) view of our American past. This produces a leftist bias in student minds against America and blindsides them to important principles when studying other subjects. While making frequent use of the word *democracy*, textbooks subtly prescribe submission to secular mentors.

Deviancy of the progressivist mindset (from the parent/taxpayer view of education) is reflected in the 1994 proposal for teaching American history. The proposal, released by the National Education Standards for U.S. History, was sent to their Improvement Council, which is part of the Federal Government Education Goals 2000 Act. Consider the following from a *Wall Street Journal* article:

Imagine an outline for the teaching of American history in which George Washington only makes a fleeting appearance and is never described as being our first president. The National Organization of Women is a noteworthy event, but the first gathering of the first Congress is not; Alexander Graham Bell, Albert Einstein, Jones Slake and the Wright brothers make no appearance at all. According to . . . [one insider] who wishes not to be named, "those who were pursuing the revisionist agenda' no longer bothered to conceal their great hatred for traditional history'" (Lynne V. Cheney, "The End of History," *The Wall Street Journal*, October 20, 1994).

The following are examples of revisionist history from research done for *The Atlantic Monthly* by the scholar Dinesh D'Souza:

Stanford University abolished its long-standing Western Culture [Judeo-Christian refinements advanced in England and America] requirement, replacing it with a program called Cultures, Ideas and Values. In practice this abolishment meant that texts such as *Plato's Republic* and *Machiavelli's Prince* would have to make way for such works as *I, Rigoberta Menchu*, the political odyssey of a Guatemalan peasant woman who discovers feminism and socialism, and Frantz Fanon's *Wretched of the Earth,* a passionate argument for violence . . .. Dartmouth College [like many] has a non-Western, but no Western, prerequisite for graduation.

New forms of criticism, now dominant in taxpayer-funded universities and teachers' colleges, are warring against traditional American education philosophy:

Houston Baker, of the University of Pennsylvania, argued that the American university suffers from a crisis of too much reading and writing. Baker emphasized the oral tradition, extolling the virtues of rap music and holding up as exemplars such groups as Public Enemy and NWA (NWA stands for "Niggas With Attitude;" the group sings about, among other things, the desirability of killing policemen). Deconstruction of the character of America's founders is justified, according to many leftists, by their concern for "multiculturalism." Significant contributions by pro-American European white males (such as American Founding Fathers) become suspect, and complex and rickety cases are built for the contributions of lesbians, Taoists, etc. Currently, 41 states . . . include some overt form of this multiculturalism [promoting hatred and bitterness between people] in their public school curriculum (Dinesh D'Souza, *The Atlantic Monthly,* March 4, 1991, pp. 52-53).

George Washington warned against the spread of divisiveness between our people in his Farewell Address. He called for Americans to set aside their cultural differences and to focus on their common heritage as sons and daughters of liberty: "With slight shades of difference, you have the same religion, manners, habits, and political principles. You have in a common cause fought and triumphed together. The independence and liberty you possess are the work of joint councils, and joint efforts . . . of common dangers, sufferings and successes." **It is precisely the promotion of the unity in our tradition, manners, habits, and principles that is being distorted or banned in the public school classroom today**. A scientific study admits as much. Professor Paul Vitz of New York University was commissioned by the United States government to conduct an extensive study of textbooks used in public schools. His findings were shocking.

Most often, liberal bias ignores the noble and focuses on the ignoble. That is, the liberals use all the exceptions as examples, implying that the exceptions should be the rule. The conclusion of the lesson may be that class hatred, stealing, and lying are not necessarily wrong. Professor Paul Vitz's study of our public school textbooks confirms this conclusion. "Over and over," he says, "we have seen that secular bias is primarily by exclusion, by leaving out the opposite (pro-moral, pro-family) position. Such a bias is the essence of harmful censorship. It is effective (brain washing of our youth) . . . because . . . it makes only the liberal, secular positions familiar and plausible."

He continues, "The study was conducted to answer two very important basic questions. Are textbooks used in public schools biased? Are they censored? The answer to both is clearly 'yes.' And the nature of the bias is clear: [moral] religion, traditional family values, and conservative political and economic positions have been reliably excluded from children's textbooks. This exclusion is particularly disturbing because it is found in a system that is paid for by taxpayers and that claims, moreover, to be committed to impartial knowledge and accuracy. A very widespread secular or liberal mindset is apparent. This mindset pervades the leadership in the world of education [textbook publishing]." (Paul Vitz, *Censorship: Evidence of Bias in Our Children's Textbooks*, Ann Arbor, Michigan, Servant Books, 1986, p. 1).

Americans believe in the shared values for responsible liberty duties and rights. Furthermore, they accept the value of government by written and permanent law rather than government by incalculable and changeable decrees which is suited to the manipulative agendas of contemporary liberals.

Public schools are no longer teaching the principles gleaned from history. Dr. William J. Bennett, former Secretary of Education, writes:

> In the late sixties and seventies we saw a sustained attack on traditional American values and the place where those values had long had a comfortable and congenial home—the local school. Many of the elite correctly understood that civilization's major task is

the upbringing of children; if they could alter the ways we reared children by changing the way we teach them, they could then alter American society to suit their view of the world. Once the traditional teachings were discredited and then removed, the vacuum was filled by faddish nonsense, and the kids (along with our nation) lost (*The Devaluing of America*, pp. 51-52).

Public school programs for multiculturalism are being compared to the brainwashing techniques used against American prisoners held captive by Communist China (Jan Mickelson, WHO radio, Des Moines, Iowa, November 19, 2001). Even scholars such as Arthur Schlesinger, Jr., whose conservatism is very sketchy, are appalled by the deception disguised as multiculturalism. Dr. Schlesinger raised his voice against this education bias in his new book, *The Disuniting of America*. In this work he echoes George Washington's call for Americans to focus and unite around founding principles rather than focusing upon what divides them (see the Bonus Book, chapter six, "American Principles." This chapter is a truth-for-our-day review of American history).

B. PUBLIC SCHOOLS ARE BIASED AGAINST THE AMERICAN FAMILY

Though never a successful parent, the government education hierarchy seeks, with taxpayer funding, to take over that role. In the 1960s, they began to use the public schools to attack the reputation of the American family. **Prior to that time OUR FAMILIES WERE STRONG.** Crime and delinquency among teenagers were low.

Families are the foundation of American life. Forces attempting to destroy the family have existed for many years. In 1848, Karl Marx attacked the family in the *Manifesto of the Communist Party*. He appealed to academia and others for the "abolition of the family." "The bourgeois clap-trap about the family and education, about the hallowed correlation of parent and child" is "disgusting." Judith Stacey, highly regarded member of the public school primary and secondary education faculty at the University of California in Davis, said: "The family' is not here to stay. All democratic people, whatever their kinship preferences, should work to hasten its demise" (quoted in "Rights and Rites," *The Washington Times*, March 29, 1993).

Public schools often promote atheistic beliefs by incorporating them into their teaching of the classics. High school English teachers twist John Steinbeck's *Grapes of Wrath* to "prove" the failure of capitalism. They re-interpret Nathaniel Hawthorne's *The Scarlet Letter* as a warning against the "cruelty" and "intolerance" of labeling anyone (even a self-professed Communist) with unfavorable terms like "leftist." Traditional family values are abandoned or ridiculed. Preference for leftist values receives enormous acclaim.

Taxpayer-funded education should be unabashedly pro-family in nature, encourage commitment to marriage, and support parental authority in the rearing of children. Upon the family unit, more than any other, stands each individual's development for strength of character and self-reliance. A key factor affecting the family is the standard for sexual behavior. Counter-culture sex education based upon "open-mindedness and free inquiry" has proven to be devastating.

The following is an education ploy which disgusted parents complain about on the editorial pages of their local newspaper. To avoid disclosure to parents and administrators by having the practice in their course outline, radical teachers get pornography on the teaching agenda by having favored students ask questions such as, "What takes place during oral sex?" and, "What is it like for lesbians to have sex?" Favored students are then considered gifted students and marked for leadership.

The *Values Clarification* handbook, a best-seller used by public schools, asks the following: tell where you stand on the subject of _____; how important are engagement rings to you?; talk about your allowance—how much you get, when and how, and whether you think it is fair; to whom would you tell you have had _____?; have you considered suicide?; do you use illegal drugs?; have you had an abortion?; your method of _____? (cited in William K. Kilpatrick, *Why Johnny Can't Tell Right From Wrong*, Simon & Shuster, New York, NY, 1992, pages 18-20).

Why are secularists so uninhibited and terroristic in their determination to control curriculum content in our schools?

When we observe what secularists do without knowing their morality and objectives, when we assume they use our own Judeo-Christian standards of decency, our conclusions about them are wrong and paralytic. From their perspective, man has no soul and God cannot exist. They think that people who believe in moral behavior, impartial and fixed law, and self-government are contaminated and, like sick animals, must be cured of their disease. Student exposure to the Creator-based ideas and the American Pledge of Allegiance is hated. This cannot be tolerated because it undermines the values monopoly which is essential for deceiving students. The secularists' logic of purifying the masses bestows upon them the righteous duty to be mean-spirited, or even worse when necessary, in order to subdue opposition and maintain control.

C. TENURE-DRIVEN SCHOOLS ARE A HAVEN FOR THOSE OPPOSED TO STUDENT-HELD MORAL FAITH

The anti-Christian bigotry emanating from public schools can be traced to the secular humanist doctrine of intolerance toward the moral religions. "Religious humanism maintains that all associations and institutions exist for the fulfillment of human life. The intelligent evaluation, transformation, CONTROL, AND DIRECTION of such associations and institutions [schools, churches, Boy Scouts, etc.] . . . **IS THE PURPOSE and program of HUMANISM**" (*Humanist Manifesto I*, 1933).

After over 200 years of Constitutional history, the Bible has been banned as a source of knowledge. It is no longer acknowledged for its greatness as a source for literature and history. The Ten Commandments ("thou shalt not steal," "thou shalt not commit adultery," "thou shalt not kill [murder]," etc.) are now inappropriate to teach our children. Added to this tyranny, curriculum writers have succeeded in displacing the primary emphasis upon the "three Rs" with their ideological agenda. While spending much less time and money for education, home-schooled children have higher test scores and win national spelling contests.

Moral Tradition vs. Secular Leftist State—It is bad enough that public schools are being used to drive a wedge between students and their parents, but captive public classrooms are also being used to impose mind-altering curriculum, which demeans the concept of faith in God and any guidelines for distinguishing between right and wrong. The following is a practice reported by the Rutherford Institute: "Elementary school children are encouraged to use the four-letter words for _____ and _____." "Students are shown a steamy film of _____. After the film is over, the boys and girls are asked to pair off and _____ is required to _____." The impact of emotions and fantasies upon the minds of youth is part of the *Final Report of the Attorney General's Commission on Pornography*, Rutledge Hill Press, Nashville, Tennessee.

The genesis of secular humanists' belief about life's origin, meaning, and purpose is the atheistic theory of evolution.

But the obligations that apply to **theistic religions** should also apply to **atheistic religions**! By refusing to admit that their faith-dependent belief is religious, secular militants hope to escape responsibility. They hope to escape the responsibility for being moral and honest and having religious tolerance, which they attach to other faiths.

> **The interests of society require the observation of those moral precepts . . . on which all [moral] relig-ions agree, for all forbid us to murder, steal, plun-der, or bear false witness and that we [government of law and justice for and by the people] should not intermeddle with the particular dogmas in which all religions differ, and which are totally unconnected with morality (Jefferson letter to James Fishback, September 27, 1809).**

The minds of students in taxpayer-funded classrooms hav-ing been or being taught to believe that the theory of evolu-tion is factual science are being assaulted by a colossal hoax. All aspects of our understanding about purpose, morality, and justice hinge upon our belief about how life began.

Dr. Michael Ruse, a leading authority on the philosophy of soft science, wrote: "Evolution is promoted by its practitio-ners as more than mere science. Evolution is an ideology, a secular religion—a full-fledged alternative to Christianity, with meaning and morality . . ... Evolution is a religion. This was true of evolution in the beginning and is true of evolu-tion today" (*National Post*, May 13, 2000).

Evolution cannot be truly tested and certainly not repeated. Consequently, it falls outside of empirical science into the realm of a philosophy or "religion," as Ruse suggests. Richard Lewontin, a leading evolutionist from Harvard, admits the following concerning the fabrication of evolu-tionary science. "Take the side of science (i.e. naturalism, Ed). In spite of patent absurdity of some of its constructs . . ..

In spite of the tolerance of the scientific community for unsubstantiated commitment to materialism . . .. Moreover, that materialism is absolute, for we cannot allow a Divine Foot in the door" (Richard Lewontin, *New York Review of Books*, January 9, 1997).

The skeptical philosophers (secularists, Darwinian teachers, etc.) claim and exercise the privilege of assuming, without proof of the very first principles of their philosophy; and yet they require, from others [theists], a proof of everything . . . They are unreasonable in both points (*U.S. Supreme Court Justice James Wilson Lectures, 1790-1791*).

All scientists do not believe in evolution as secular militants argue. The study of historian Edward J. Larson of the University of Georgia, Athens, suggests that only 45 percent of scientists do not believe in God. This compares with 41.5 percent in a survey done in 1916 ("Scientists' Belief in God Stable Since 1916," *Daily Tribune*, Ames, Iowa, April 4, 1997).

Only about 1.3 percent of the people in America are public school teachers (kindergarten through high school). The teacher population in geology and biology, which are heavily Darwinian, along with teachers in the soft sciences (social and mixed studies) would be close to half of 1 percent of the American population. Textbooks in the soft sciences teach the secular worldview, but probably no more than 5 percent of teachers in the soft sciences are themselves secular militants. All told, leftist missionaries in our primary and secondary schools, along with militants in the universities, the media, textbook writers, movie makers, and those in control of wealthy foundations, are probably no more than 2.5 percent of the population in America. **With the pretense of authority and access to immature youth in captive government classrooms, however, they wield an enormous anti-American, anti-morality weapon.**

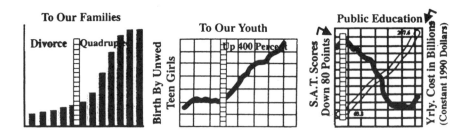

marks 1962 when, after 175 years of constitutional history, a secular minority succeeded in leveraging the God of creation, moral faith, and the Bible out of our schools.

These teachers must embody the same selfless dedication as the most rabid fundamentalist preachers, for they will be ministers of another sort, utilizing a classroom instead of a pulpit to convey humanist values in whatever subject they teach, regardless of the education level—preschool, daycare or large state university. The classroom must and will become an area of conflict between the old and the new—the rotting corpse of Christianity, together with its adjacent evils and misery and the new faith of Humanism, resident in its promise of a world in which the never-realized Christian idea of "Love Thy Neighbor" will finally be achieved (*The Humanist*, January/February 1983).

D. TAXPAYER-FUNDED SCHOOLS ARE ALSO BEING USED TO ATTACK THE ADVOCACY OF MORAL FAITH BY PRIVATE SECTOR ORGANIZATIONS

In addition to being facilitators for the exploitation of youthful minds with mind-altering instruction, our schools are being used to attack the freedom of God-honoring organizations which function in the non-government sector. This includes attacks against the Boy Scout organization and 4-H programs, service clubs, businesses, farmers' markets, community fund allocations, the Salvation Army, churches and synagogues:

> Speakers included James Audry, strong supporter of the religious left and a founder of "the American Way, a liberal advocacy group in Washington, D.C." and Angie King, president of the Iowa State Education Association Union. Attacking the right of citizens to influence values taught in public schools as if the moral religions and morality were un-American, Audry told Iowa State Education Association delegates, "What I call being a Christian and what they call being a Christian are two different things" ("Religious Right Rapped by Educators," *Daily Tribune*, Ames, Iowa, April 3, 1993).

> Ron Shimkus, who holds what he calls a "traditional Judeo-Christian" view in opposition to homosexuality, has spoken to high school students and others about homosexuality alongside Keith Schrag, whom Shimkus describes as "an aggressive advocate of

homosexual rights." The two . . . were invited to the 4-H conference for a similar presentation. When Shimkus called to confirm, 4-H officials told him they had decided to withdraw the invitation and have only Keith Schrag facilitate a discussion of homosexuality, Shimkus said ("Parents Complain That [Iowa State University Education Extension] 4-H Seminars Advocate Gay Lifestyle," *Daily Tribune*, Ames, Iowa, May 6, 1993).

Ron Shimkus, who holds what he calls a "traditional Judeo-Christian" view of family and sex was removed from the 4-H seminar ("4-H Officials Yank Invite From Speaker," *Daily Tribune*, Ames, Iowa, June 14, 1993).

Dr. John Dewey, acknowledged by educators to be the father of modern day public education, was an admirer of Margaret Sanger, Humanist of the Year in

Dr. John Dewey presents Margaret Sanger with
American Women's Association Medal - 1932

1967 and a founder of Planned Parenthood. Dr. Mary Calderone and Faye Wattleton served in key positions in Planned Parenthood. Sanger founded the publication *The Woman Rebel,* whose slogan was "No Gods! No Masters!" Her first edition denounced marriage as a "degenerate institution" and sexual modesty as "obscene prudery." In 1964, Dr. Mary Calderone left her position as medical director for Planned Parenthood and founded the organization called Sex Information and Educational Council of the United States (SIECUS). Dr. Calderone also served as a Director of the United Nation's World Health Organization. The slogan of WHO is "One World Through Mental Health" (from *Legacy of Planned Parenthood* by George Grant).

Not only are secular militants using their position as public school employees to denigrate and suppress calls for morality as the public norm, but they are also seeking to lower the standards essential in law to make dishonesty, fraud, and violence unprofitable. Stanford University professor Thomas Sowell points out, "Too many people in the education establishment, at all levels, treat education as the continuation of leftist ideological crusades" (*Boston Herald*, May 30, 1992). This is especially true of the "leaders" in public school education—members of the National Education Association (NEA). The NEA has aligned itself with the liberal agenda on virtually every issue. William J. Bennett catalogs their folly:

The modern-day NEA is primarily a political action organization. It routinely takes liberal and even left wing stands on political candidates and on many national and international affairs. In recent years the union's Representative Assembly went on record in favor of teacher strikes; school-based clinics dispensing contraceptives; gay rights. It has voted against merit pay for teachers; parental choice; voluntary school prayer; home schooling; English as the official language; drug, alcohol, and AIDS testing; the nomination of Judge Robert Bork to the Supreme Court (Dr. William Bennett, *The Devaluing of America,* Summit Books, New York, 1992, p. 48).

E. SECULAR TOTALITARIANS SEEK TO JUSTIFY AN OPPRESSIVE EDUCATION TAX

A large body of empirical evidence on the effects of the resources on student achievement already exist. It overwhelmingly shows that, at given spending levels, an increase in resources does not generally raise educational performance. Studies summarized by Eric Hanushek of the Hoover Institute have shown a lack of a strong relationship between resources and performance within the United States, within developing countries, and among (other) countries . . . [Researchers] at the Kiel Institute of World Economics have found no systematic relationship between resources and performance across time within most countries in the Organization for Economic Cooperation and Development (report from the Hoover Institute, October 30, 2001).

Since 1960, our population has increased 41 percent. Adjusted for inflation, spending on primary and secondary education has increased over 225 percent (not 41 percent). Costs per student for public elementary and secondary schools, in constant 1990 dollars, had nearly tripled by year 2000. The highest tax of all is a 560 percent increase in violent crime, more than a 400 percent increase in illegitimate births and a 200 percent rise in teen suicides. Welfare costs, adjusted for inflation, increased 630 percent. The drug and alcohol problem continues unabated. Prior to 1960, these problems were minimal (data from the U.S. Department of Education and The Heritage Foundation).

Family Time Famine . . . many mothers have felt compelled to join the work force to make ends meet . . .. A 1988 *USA Today* survey found that 73 percent of two-parent families would choose to have one parent remain at home full-time to care for their children "if money were not an issue" (The Thomas A. Roe Institute for Economic Policy Studies, *Reducing the Crushing Tax Burden on America's Families,* cited by The Heritage Foundation).

CONCLUSION

The greatness of American values for education is grounded in the lessons learned over 4,000 years of recorded history. Citizens at the grassroots—conservatives, moderates, and liberals—are vested with the authority to establish a consensus for public policy. Religious tolerance, along with citizen dialogue and debate, becomes the basis for a consensus for public policy.

The content of education in the soft sciences which springs from leftists "**faith in openmindedness and free inquiry**" is not an adaptation of the education upon which responsible liberty depends. It is the sworn enemy of and is alien to American traditions and values. The American education philosophy succeeded because it protected the minds of students from the advocates of moral defilement, taught universal values, and insisted that students learn the basics. Simply stated, there are certain standards for what students should not learn as well as some socially indispensable principles which must be taught.

Secular militants achieve leadership positions by falsifying their intent and proceed from there to accomplish their objectives. There are perhaps better estimates, but these people are something like 3.5 percent of the American population. When what they are doing comes to light, they submit to citizen outrage by backing up one step. When the public storm settles down, they simply return to their ways and take two more steps toward their goals.

The Commission on Excellence in Education was right when it compared the harm being done to America through public schools to **what we could expect from "war" by an "unfriendly" foreign power**. The problem, though, is not with hard sciences such as math, physics, chemistry, engineering, *et cetera.*

Our problem comes from the religio/social/political sciences which are susceptible to misrepresentation by textbook writers and teachers. What has happened could be compared to the story of the Trogan Horse. The people of Troy pulled a wooden horse into their city, not realizing that enemy soldiers were hidden in the hollow of the horse. Instead of going to Americans and seeking an amendment to the *Constitution* through constitutional means, collectivist liberals are subverting the representative process and undermining the *Constitution of the United States*. By deceptively misrepresenting the *Bill of Rights* (restrictions on government), and, through the exercise of rudeness and militancy, they now control education for the soft sciences in most of the universities and lower level public schools. They are attacking the heart of America and clearly fit the description of the enemies spoken of by the U. S. Commission on Excellence in Education.

The premature deaths of tens of thousands of 18- to 44-year-olds from suicides, sexually transmitted diseases, and drugs, now attributable to the takeover of education by secular militants, are justified by the militants' goal to alter our thinking and control our lives. How much this loss exceeds the loss of life inflicted upon America on September 11, 2001, will never be known.

There are three serious barriers which prevent the American public and school administrators from regaining control of the soft science sector of education.

1. Teachers' unions that negotiate with school administrators and regents, or school boards, have become an extension of government with more power than most other departments of government and practically no accountability to the people. Political force garnered by leftist professors and lawyers have, in this writer's opinion, succeeded in turning the *Bill of Rights* against the people it was established to protect. The original intent of the *Bill of Rights* places specific limits upon government, lest it be used by tyrants to undermine the authority and control levers that the people must have to keep government power in submission (working in the people's interest). In this instance, the government (teachers' unions and tenure laws) has become sovereign over the people's right to control what is taught in the religio/social/political sciences.

We have too many judges appointed who refuse to believe that the *Constitution* means what it says.

With the help of the American Association of University Professors and American Civil Liberties Union lawyers, the people's chain of command that is essential for superintending what is taught has been undermined. The teachers' employment rights, which are now superior to taxpayer citizen rights, empower militants to teach over the objections of the American people. In other words, the power in government held by the leftists' special interests has grown and now exceeds the power of the people who foot the bills and whose children are on the losing end (see page 49 of the previous chapter).

2. The atheistic humanist elites are using the hard science sector of our universities for fund raising credibility and as a shield. When humanists in the soft sciences experience meaningful opposition from school administrators, they may threaten a teachers' strike or the school's accreditation. This could bring instruction in the hard

sciences to a halt so, in order to avoid a stoppage, they are inclined to let the leftists have their way in dealing with the administration. When the public hears that the accreditation of such and such university is in jeopardy, the reputation of the entire university and its administration is harmed. All of this is a very real threat which authorities cannot ignore while trying to reign in secular militants in the soft sciences.

We now quote the Iowa Civil Liberties Union (ICLU), translated by this writer as the un-civil liberties union, speak on the subject. In their book, *Freedom In Iowa,* published in 1977 by the Iowa State University Press, they expressed their happiness with the liberal influence of the presidents on the operation of all three Iowa universities. The Iowa Civil Liberties Union referred to the presidents as "devoted" supporters of the ICLU agenda and "honored" them for this.

Following the 1970 publication of the uniform rules of personal conduct for faculty and students by the Iowa Board of Regents, the ICLU, along with the leftist American Association of University Professors (AAUP), did not appear to be very happy. The ICLU response was a not-too-veiled threat of reprisal.

Their response reflected the political power generated by a miniscule minority of professors and teachers who are well organized and coordinated at both the nationwide and local levels:

> The book *Freedom In Iowa,* published by the Iowa State University Press, states the following on pages 152-153. "The ICLU supports the recent statement by the American Civil Liberties Union on 'Academic Freedom and Civil Liberties of Students in Colleges and Universities.' This report urges that 'students should participate fully and effectively in formulating and

adjudicating college regulations governing student conduct' and further states that 'regulations governing demonstrations should be made by a committee of administrators, representative faculty and democratically selected students.' Failure of the Regents to seek participation of representatives of the various university constituents may seriously jeopardize relationships between the Regents and the persons [faculty and students] they seek to govern."

The ICLU continued, "Serious concern must be expressed about the effect that the Regents' Rules may have upon established rules and procedures regarding academic tenure. [The Regents] ". . . appear to bypass those procedures which have been formulated by the American Association of University Professors for the hearing of cases involving the dismissal of tenured faculty. These American Associations of University Professors principles (1940 Statement on Academic Freedom) have been accepted by all three state universities and must be considered as part of the contractural relationship between the university and the individual professor on tenure. The establishment of new procedures and contractural arrangements [by the Regents] raises serious questions about the continued accreditation of the universities" (pages 153-154).

3. Teacher training faculty, textbook and curriculum review committees, teacher licensing criteria, and student grading systems are wholly compromised. The parent/taxpayer authority chain of command is compromised by the inclusion of determined militants who are supported by the ACLU and AAUP in these echelons intended to direct education in the public interest.

It is this type of collusion which brought the European

public to its knees in Medieval Europe. Separating the powers of government from the Latin Church that had charge over education eventually solved that problem. The collectivist hierarchy was no longer leveraged over the people by the power of government. The corruption of education in the soft sciences came to a halt as education became the **function of competing, non-government, citizen choice entities.**

Following such a separation, government institutions offering diploma programs in the hard sciences would honor a soft science and historical studies diploma from any number of citizen choice, privately funded institutions.

Militant secularists are radically opposed to separation of manipulatable soft sciences instruction from government empowered (tenure guarantees) because others will be on a par and students will hear the truth about American history.

> "The growth and use . . . by one special interest group of political power which has no effective check is not the fault primarily of those who achieve the power, for it is their right to try. Rather, the fault is principally on the part of those who, by their inactivity and silence, allowed it to happen" (from a citizen action booklet, Chamber of Commerce of the United States, 1980).

This writer is guardedly optimistic. The children who are taught by moms who are free of any government teacher training are much better educated. The truth is getting out. **Do what you can to help! Like the public school teachers who are taking their own children out of government (public) schools by the thousands, Americans are accepting responsibility by informing others and taking strong measures on behalf of their treasured ideals that are under siege.**

Chapter Six

American Principles

novus ordo seclorum, meaning
"A NEW ORDER OF THE AGES"
The Great Seal of the United States of America

A definite, unique and specific American philosophy of government does exist. Under the influence of that philosophy, our nation became the overwhelming choice of people from throughout the world. Chief among the foundations of the American philosophy is the belief that man is the beneficiary of human rights which are superior to secular claims, government, and things material.

Therefore, governments serve as a tool under the direction of the people for the preservation of their unalienable God-given rights. This philosophy is an indivisible whole and any compromise in upholding its principles destroys its functionality. The bricks and mortar of this unique American philosophy are detailed in the *Declaration of Independence.*

Where have the great movers of needed cultural change turned? In addition to the Bible, what did they talk about? What was the theme of the two contrasting leaders for significant change, Abraham Lincoln and Martin Luther King, Jr.? It was the language of the *Declaration of Independence,* unanimously approved by the Continental Congress in the late afternoon of July 4, 1776. This *Declaration,* which came upon the world scene like an unrelenting tide, is the all-sufficient basis for renewal today.

Where did American Principles originate? America's Founding Fathers had vision. They saw the potential for human dignity in a setting of responsible choices, awareness of human history, and the principles in the Bible.

Professor Donald S. Lutes of the University of Houston describes a ten-year study in which he and others assembled the writings and deliberations of the American Founding Fathers. The study brought into focus important historical facts about the near miraculous design of our *Constitution.* Aside from quotations from the Bible used by the Founding Fathers, the three men quoted most often were Montesquieu, Blackstone, and Locke.

The Bible was quoted three times more often than were these three men combined. Thirty-four percent of all the quotes used by our Founding Fathers came directly from the Old and New Testament books.

Furthermore, sixty percent of the references to opinions of others were drawn from the Bible. The most frequently quoted was the Hebrew book Deuteronomy in the Old Testament. The concept of three branches of government (administrative, legislative, and judicial) for the *Constitution* was found in Isaiah 33:22. The extremely important "separation of powers" principle came from Jeremiah 17 (Donald S. Lutes, *Origins of the American Constitutionals*, Louisiana State University Press, 1988).

Mankind has the choice of two fundamentally different worldviews or opinions about the truth or reality. The Judeo-Christian worldview arises out of a belief in the infinite God Who created man in His own image. The focus of the Bible, going back over 4,000 years, is history and God's role on behalf of mankind. Every person is seen by God to be of infinitely precious value and has the unique spiritual capacity to be guided by and work with God. The other worldview places man at the helm. Having rejected God, those who embrace this worldview tend to proceed in a way that reflects the incalculable and changeable decrees of worldly men. The value of life becomes the arbitrary choice of the hierarchy that manages to be in control of the knowledge centers and law at any given time. This secular worldview has no basis whatsoever for unalienable human rights which cause restrictions to be placed on government activities.

To preserve the right of the American people to control the distribution of power in the government they established, citizens must maintain a firm understanding of the reality upon which their liberty is based. To serve effectively on behalf of responsible liberty, the procedures for government must take into account human nature which is not the progression to perfection that atheists claim.

William Ellery Channing wrote:

> Erase all thought and fear of God from a community, and [the emotions of] selfishness and sensuality would absorb the whole man. Appetite knowing no restraint, and poverty and suffering having no solace or hope, man would trample in scorn on the restraints of human laws. Virtue, duty, principle would be

mocked and scorned as unmeaning sounds. A sordid self-interest would supplant every feeling [emotion], and man would become . . . a companion of brutes. (Channing quotation from 1820, "The Great Doctrine of Retribution: The Founders' Views of the Social Utility of [moral] Religion," cited by James Hutson in a presentation to the John Courtney Murray Seminar at the American Enterprise Institute, June 6, 2000).

Seriousness in preserving the original intent of the *American Constitution* is the difference between responsible liberty for the people and imperial license which leads to learning impoverishment and exploitation. How do the people protect themselves from deception and exploitation?

The historians, Will and Ariel Durant, pointed out the early recognition of the very important procedural dichotomy in *Solon of Athens*: translated "government by written and permanent law" versus "government by incalculable and changeable decrees" (Will and Ariel Durant, *The Story of Civilization*, vol. II, *The Life of Greece*, published 1939).

Those who think a third choice for governing exists do not understand the meaning of the words *permanent law* and *changeable decrees. Solon of Athens* had not identified the God of Creation, but he understood the ever-present existence of men who are masters of deception and determined to exploit others.

The definition of government:

> **Government by and for the people** is a tertiary force instituted by God. The power exercised by government comes from the people when they covenant together to share a small portion of their right as individuals to use force for the protection of their own property and the liberty essential for the pursuit of happiness.

Government functions properly when the citizens fulfill their covenant responsibilities. It is indispensable that new generations be taught and understand the real world of cause and effect. By keeping informed on current issues, they can help bring the body politic to a consensus for laws which honor God and responsible behavior. There is a common need for sharing in the maintenance of highways, for instance, and instituting laws which will keep thieves out of the corncrib and see to it that the food sold in the grocery store is safe to eat. It is very important, however, that government be limited. Religious and soft science education must be left to the private sector, free from any monopoly, including the misuse of government influence on behalf of one sect or another over knowledge dissemination.

Consistent with this prohibition, courts are responsible for protecting the right of communities that choose to encourage voluntary prayer and honor toward the non-sectarian God of Creation in a democratic way. Traditionally in America, leaders from the various local Christian churches have been invited to present moral truth from the Bible to students in taxpayer-funded schools.

As late as 1940, the National Education Association published the booklet, *A Golden Treasury From The BIBLE*. It included the Lord's Prayer, the Golden Rule, the Ten Commandments, and many other verses instructive for personal growth. The government purchased Bibles for soldiers in World War II and promoted Bible distribution in more recent wars. Our money and national monuments such as the Supreme Court building are scripted to honor God.

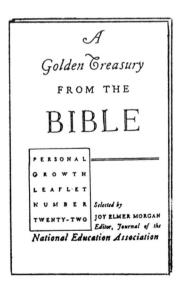

> Because of the sometimes brutal determination of man and his propensity to want control over the lives and property of others, care must be taken to maintain the **return-to-citizen authority** procedures.

One of the **return-to-citizen authority** procedures is citizen jury, adopted effectively from the Bible (Matthew 18:15-17) by William Penn. Another is the requirement that those employed to legislate and administer public policy must stand frequently in competition with others for re-election. The significance of government by written and permanent law instead of government by incalculable and changeable decrees is, of course, because of man's sin-prone nature.

Buffered from intrigue and deception by insisting on government by written and permanent law, the proponents of moral religions experience the blessings that flow from the practice of biblical absolutes demonstrated throughout human history. This contrasts from the followers of the many little gods whose outcomes are the natural consequence of emotions and religio/social relativism.

Historically, men yielding to their own selfish instincts wrestle power (the lever of government) from control by the people while proclaiming religious and/or intellectual superiority. They then use the power of taxation to sustain and fulfill their godless rights-granting agenda. Citizens who control their government by permanent laws of a principled nature, as intended by the *American Constitution*, have little difficulty keeping government power in submission. A **return-to-citizen authority** procedure that needs to be fiercely upheld is the requirement that interpretations which disagree with *Constitution* originalism be submitted to a vote by the people to determine their usability.

The following is excerpted from William Blackstone's writings on the law. It is being included because his explanation is so helpful to understanding American jurisprudence. Blackstone outlined the Higher Authority basis for government on pages 38-40 of Volume I of his *Commentaries on the Laws of England* (1765-1769). Abraham Lincoln and many other law students used Blackstone's textbooks until around 1920. Blackstone stated:

> Law, in its most general and comprehensive sense, signifies a rule of action; whether animate, or inanimate, rational or irrational. And it is that rule of action which is prescribed by some superior, and which the inferior is bound to obey.
>
> Thus when the Supreme Being formed the universe and created matter out of nothing, He impressed certain principles upon that matter, from which it can never depart . . . [Blackstone goes on to say the same thing about vegetable and animal life and all branches of economy, human action, and conduct]. "[They] are not left to chance or the will of the creature itself, but are performed in a wondrous involuntary manner, and guided by unerring rules laid down by the great Creator. That is, the precepts by which man, the noblest of all sublunary [under the stars] beings, a creature endowed with both reason and freewill, is commanded to make use of those faculties in general regulation of his [or her] behavior.
>
> A being, independent of any other [than his Creator], has no rule to pursue, but such as he prescribes to himself [or that of some politically correct demagogue]; but a state of dependence will inevitably oblige the inferior [if he is to have a good life] to take the will of him, on whom he depends [the Creator], as a rule of his conduct.
>
> This will of his maker is called the law of nature [or of God's Creation]. For as God, when He created matter, and endued it with a principle of mobility, established certain rules for the perpetual direction of

that motion; so, when He created man, and endued him with freewill to conduct himself in all parts of life, He laid down certain immutable [and totally reliable] laws [reflective] of human nature, whereby that freewill is in some degree regulated and restrained [for the sake of civil decency], and gave him also the faculty of reason to discover the [beneficial] purport of those laws.

Considering the Creator only as a being of infinite power, He was able unquestionably to have prescribed whatever laws He pleased to His creature, man, however unjust or severe. But as He is also a being of infinite *wisdom*, He has laid down only such laws as were founded in those relations of justice, that existed in the nature of things antecedent [prior] to any positive precept. These are the eternal, immutable laws of good and evil, to which the Creator himself in all his dispensations conforms; and which He has enabled human reason to discover, so far as they are necessary for the conduct of human actions. **Such among others are these principles** [for the avoidance of evil, its deception and harmful outcomes]: **that we should live honestly, should hurt nobody, and should render to every one its [moral] due**; to which [those] three general precepts justification has reduced the whole doctrine of law" (bold added for emphasis).

The choice of the Higher Authority impartial Creator over some humanistic presupposition as the basis for American legal and political philosophy is both historically accurate and a necessary foundation for responsible liberty in the future.

Illustrative of the foolishness of self-enamored men, after two world wars and assorted strifes coming out of Europe, Germany in particular, liberals in America turned to European secularism for what is called higher criticism.

Secure on our campuses from opposing points of view, these professors are discrediting the Hebrew-Christian Bible, influencing textbook writers and students. They have succeeded in influencing the character and methods for interpreting history and behavioral instruction. The deceptions of Communism and Darwinian evolution pass through their filter. "In God We Trust" is censored from academically approved literature and dialogue. Their efforts continue because, as they well know, people who learn the truth about the Creator-based worldview become self reliant and have no need of, and strongly object to, elitist imperialism.

> See we not plainly that obedience of creatures unto the Law of Nature [reality of Creation] is the stay of the whole world? . . . Now the due observation of this law which Reason [based upon God's Word] teaches us, cannot but be effectual unto their good that observe the same. For we see the whole world and each part thereof so compacted, that as long as each thing performs only that work which is natural unto it, it thereby preserves both other things, and also itself (Thomas Hooker, 1554-1600, *Of the Laws of Ecclesiastical Polity*).

Leftist academia stirs up the fear of the church-state marriage, which caused centuries of thought control and subjugation in medieval Europe. It is done as a ploy to hide their drive for a more harmful marriage of atheistic ideology and government which leads with certainty to emotional and spiritual deprivation.

Contemporary liberals justify control over what they teach in the behavioral courses because their belief about life's origin is, as they deceptively imply, "hard science." The truth is that their faith in Darwinian evolution for life's origin is every bit as faith-dependent and religious as the Judeo-Christian presupposition. For them, teaching students about responsible liberty and "One Nation Under God" is intolerable. As late as June 19, 1961, the Supreme Court defined Humanism as religion (Torcaso v. Wakins). The scientist Dr. Soren Lovtrup, in his book on Darwinism, spoke for knowledgeable and honest scientists when he said, "I believe that one day the Darwinian myth will be ranked the greatest deceit in the history of science."

Liberals' unyielding insistence on the "living" interpretation of our *Constitution* is understandable. The utility of their godless worldview is tied to changeable decrees. They require the margin of freedom (government by incalculable and changeable decrees), inherent in a living *Constitution*. With every muscle in their brain, pen, and mouth, contemporary liberals will deny this, but it is the rejection of *Constitution* originalism which empowers ambiguity and concealment of their supremacist goals.

There is a truth very relevant at this time in history which needs to be broadcast from the housetops: **both the God-honoring and the God-rejecting beliefs about reality are faith-based religious assumptions.** Policy decisions for government and for training new generations flow from a presupposition about life's origin, meaning, and purpose. This truth is rooted in the fact that the most powerful human drive for social/political action comes from deeply held faith regarding the origin, meaning, and purpose of life. **It is up to regular people in America to bypass academia and make room in the dictionaries for the two different religions—moral religions which are based upon the non-sectarian God of the universe, and the unprincipled religions (those that reject impartial laws based upon established knowledge which includes moral absolutes).**

Quoting from the Grand Jury Presentment, chapter four of this book—In place of established knowledge, they [contemporary liberals] want relativism as the accepted [approach to education]. Relativism . . . refers to the denial of absolutes and puts evil on a par with discerned truth as a legitimate teaching subject. Such a position on fundamental tenets raises a very interesting question. If the desirability of sexual virtue and undesirability of overnight co-habitation in single student dorms is as they say a matter of opinion, if in fact sexual virtue and many other tenets such as basic honesty are not established knowledge suitable for classroom doctrine—what is the good of having humanities courses at all? When a radical teacher lectures, what is he accomplishing with taxpayers' money?

When the God of Creation is censored from the ideas presented to students and public dialog, God moves out of the picture. But the intensity and severity of the consequences of rejecting God's law, or the laws of nature, are not reduced. The consequences for violations remain the outcomes man must bear.

Cecil B. DeMille, in an address at Baylor University on October 12, 1957, said, "The [American] principle of separation of church and state has never meant and need never mean the exclusion of moral and religious values from education or the exiling of God from our national life. If you believe that it does mean that, you must cut out . . . 'endowed by their Creator with certain unalienable rights' . . . and when you cut that out, you have cut out the heart that pumps the lifeblood of liberty through the nation's veins. If men will not be ruled by God [principles advanced by trust in God], they will . . . certainly be ruled by tyrants . . . But if we believe, as did the Founding Fathers, that the law of God [truth in reality] is and must always be an American ideal, then it is worth the giving of the last ounce of your strength, the last drop of your blood, and the last breath of our lives."

The emotional charge of liberals is that conservatives are conspiring to dictate public policy. This is not true and the liberals know it. Truth thrives upon the competition of ideas. What conservatives are insisting upon is the freedom to have a voice in the debate and transmission of ideas.

The right to hear competing ideas is indispensable. Tens of millions of public school students, soon to be voters, are being dumbed down by a godless, distorted view of American history. They are not being told about "In God We Trust" and the importance of preserving the original intent of the *Constitution*.

> Secular militants cannot afford to teach history because it exposes their core belief and vision for a hedonistic, existentialist America in which there is no established knowledge from the past for our youth to learn and no future except what atheists/secular militants determine. What distinguishes contemporary liberals is their militant intolerance for any program or person who holds to the Judeo-Christian worldview.

People who yield to arguments for a changeable decree type of *Constitution*, or as called "living *Constitution*," soon become victims of manipulation, and government employees become masters. The situation in government (public) education where a godless Darwinian presupposition monopoly now exists is an example. This clear violation of the will of the people occurred when judges shamelessly violated the *Constitution* by flaunting the exclusive and sacred right of the people. This instance is later described in detail.

Historians tell us that C. C. Langdell, a new Dean at Harvard Law School, started the detachment from the Judeo-Christian legal tradition outlined by Blackstone and others. Beginning in the 1890s, Langdell emphasized case method to the detriment of constitutional intent. Consequently, many law graduates do not appreciate the Judeo-Christian basis for government by written and permanent law and their relevance to preserving responsible liberty. The nature of case method with its drifting anchorage opened the door for judges who are independent from recall by the people to fabricate law arbitrarily.

Thomas Paine, Thomas Jefferson, and Benjamin Franklin were not the deist friends of secularism! Michael Novak, in his excellent book, *On Two Wings,* emphasizes the God-honoring beliefs of these men. Though not a Biblicist, Paine believed in God and the inevitable nature of righteous judgment. He not only recognized the source of moral carnage in France, he went there in 1786 as a champion of responsible liberty and campaigned against atheism.

Hardly a deist, Jefferson wrote the God-honoring premise for American law into the *Declaration of Independence* and said the following about the ultimate effect of secularism upon the souls of slaves and those who enslave:

> And can the liberties of a nation be thought secure when we have removed their only firm basis, a conviction in the minds of the people that these liberties are a gift of God? That they are not violated but with His wrath? Indeed I tremble for my country when I reflect that God is just: that His justice cannot sleep forever.

Ben Franklin believed that God cares and blesses those who look to Him for wisdom. He promoted the employment of chaplains for government service. When the debate over the words to be used in the *Constitution* brought the work of the delegates to an impasse, Franklin called Congress to its knees in prayer:

> In this situation of this Assembly, groping as it were in the dark to find political truth, and scarce able to distinguish it when presented to us, how has it happened, sir, that we have not hitherto once thought of humbly applying to the Father of Lights to illuminate our understanding? Our prayers [during the recent war], sir, were heard, and they were graciously answered. To that kind providence we owe this happy opportunity of consulting in peace on the means of establishing our future felicity [through a truth-based *Constitution*]. And have we forgotten

that powerful friend? Or do we imagine that we no longer need his assistance? I have lived, sir, a long time, and the longer I live, the more convincing proofs I see of this truth, *that God governs in the affairs of men.* And if a sparrow cannot fall to the ground without His notice, is it probable that an empire can rise without His aid? We have been assured, sir, in the sacred writing, that *'except the Lord build the house, they labor in vain that build it.'*

I therefore beg leave to move—that henceforth prayers imploring the assistance of Heaven, and its blessings on our deliberations, be held in this Assembly every morning before we proceed to business, and that one or more of the clergy of this city be requested to officiate in that service.

The names for God used in the *Declaration of Independence,* upon which our *Constitution* and the *Northwest Ordinance* for new states are based, reflect the authority and character of God. The outcomes that flow from man's choices do so according to "The Laws of Nature and of **Nature's God**," our **Lawgiver**. Individuals are "endowed by their **Creator** with certain unalienable Rights." We appealed "to the **Supreme Judge** of the world for the rectitude of our intentions." "And for the support of this Declaration, with a firm reliance on the Protection of **Divine Providence,** we mutually pledge to each other our Lives, our Fortunes and our sacred Honor." Unlike the *Constitution,* the *Declaration of Independence* includes no provision for its own amending. The reason is clear. (The quotations include portions from the *Declaration* adopted by Congress.)

Accommodating the wishes of contemporary liberals guarantees the deceptive imposition of rule by incalculable and changeable decrees. Negotiating with liberals is no more effective than talking to a hollow stump. They deny that there is a spiritual and just moral power, but they will never displace that power.

No one doubts the right of those who want atheism (godless humanism) as the basis for education when they pursue their goal as private citizens and at their own expense. In fact, it is good to have a few of them around. We want to do what is right and their persistent disagreement sharpens our focus. To tax citizens for funding the salaries of tenured teachers in a compulsory education system is no less a guarantee for the incubation of evil than occurred in medieval Europe. Consequently, we see the breakdown of the family and the escalation in the rate of crime and death among American youth since 1965.

The Soviet Union, with imposing armed enforcers and great universities, made a Herculean effort to displace the spiritual nature of man. Soviets put Sputnik in the sky for all to see. Their universities excelled in the physical sciences but taught the one-sided atheistic worldview. Proclaiming the Darwinian theory of evolution to be the foundation for human progress, their nation, the workers paradise that really never was, fell apart.

Alleged to be uplifting, "openmindedness" (explained in chapter five) and evolution's moral relativism are taught to American youth. They have deliberately pushed aside "In God We Trust" and character training. Fourteen-year-olds having babies and killing each other, though, do not advance the cause of liberty and happiness. Eighteen-year-olds having AIDS and getting diplomas that they cannot read is not the stuff of national greatness.

The World Trade Center Towers, with their deep foundations and magnificent superstructures, symbolized the benefits of the hard sciences to progress in America. Men in rebellion against the laws of God brought the Towers down!

THE VERY SURE FOUNDATION

Judges, professors, textbook writers, and others alleging civil liberty concerns who claim that the *Declaration of Independence* is not a basis in law for the development of our *Constitution* are dead wrong.

In late afternoon of July 4, 1776, the Continental Congress unanimously approved the language for the *Declaration of Independence*. It was transcribed to be more easily read, and when it was signed by delegates beginning August 2, 1776, the premise that all men "are endowed by their Creator with certain unalienable Rights" became the official justification for government-related decisions. This law severed ties to England, and the thirteen colonies became states. The *Declaration* is the most inclusive brief that documents the American philosophy for government. With the *Declaration* we have our definitions of justice and liberty. The primary goal of the law is to protect liberty (God-given unalienable rights).

James Wilson was one of six men who signed both the *Declaration of Independence* and the *Constitution*. His contribution to the deliberations of the *Federal Constitution* was second only to James Madison's. As recently as 1964, Wilson's writings were used by the Supreme Court as authority for requiring equal apportioning of congressional districts throughout America.

Addressing the Pennsylvania Ratifying Convention, Wilson stated, "I beg to read a few words from *the Declaration of Independence* made by the representatives of the United States, and recognized by the whole Union." He concluded, "This is the broad basis on which our independence was placed; on the same certain and solid foundation this [*United States Constitution*] system is erected:

WHEN IN THE COURSE of human events, it becomes necessary for one people to dissolve the political bands which have connected them with another, and to assume among the powers of the earth, the separate and equal station to which the Laws of Nature and of Nature's God entitle them, a decent respect to the opinions of mankind requires that they should declare the causes which impel them to the separation.

We hold these truths to be self-evident, that all men are created equal, that they are endowed by their Creator with certain unalienable Rights, that among these are Life, Liberty and the pursuit of Happiness. That to secure these rights, Governments are instituted among Men, deriving their just powers from the consent of the governed. That whenever any Form of Government becomes destructive of these ends, it is the Right of the People to alter or to abolish it, and to institute new Government, laying its foundation on such principles and organizing its powers in such form, as to them shall seem most likely to effect their Safety and Happiness.

Henry Steele Commanger, eminent historian of the 20th century, focused on the *Declaration* as the source of America's unique principles of government, describing a new political system for the vindication of God-given rights as being of "matchless logic" and "permanent" rather than "transient" value. (*Thomas Jefferson: The Man, His World, His Influence*, G. P. Putnam, New York, 1974)

The *United States Code Annotated*, under the heading "The Organic Laws of the United States of America," lists our significant governmental instruments: the *Declaration of Independence*, the *Articles of Confederation*, the *Constitution* and the *Northwest Ordinance*. The *Northwest Ordinance* is the blueprint in law for administering the lands west of the Allegheny Mountains and northwest of the Ohio River.

The *Northwest Ordinance* is a most important post-*Declaration of Independence* legislation passed by the Continental Congress, which had struggled under the weak *Articles of Confederation* (1781-1789). The *Ordinance* guaranteed that inhabitants of the Northwest Territory, and states created therein, would have the same rights and privileges enjoyed by citizens in the original thirteen states. The most important features were in Articles III, V and VI. These articles provided a government organization formula with a moral, religious foundation and prohibited the practice of slavery in the new states. Thomas Jefferson had drafted the *Ordinance* earlier in 1784. The Continental Congress passed it on July 13, 1787, while the nation was still operating under the *Articles of Confederation*. By virtue of this *Ordinance*, the declaration "that all men are created equal" and "are endowed by their Creator with certain unalienable rights" had an enforcement mandate. Article III states, "**Religion, morality, the happiness of mankind, schools and the means of education shall forever be encouraged.**" This Article is not ambiguous.

The unworkable *Articles of Confederation* (1781) were replaced by the stronger national government in 1789. Ten amendments prohibiting the use of government power in violation of Creator-endowed citizen rights were agreed upon. This was necessary in order to overcome objections and obtain ratification of the new *Constitution* by the people in the thirteen states. **The importance of originalism in the preservation of the *Constitution* is morally and legally bound because ratification of the new *Constitution* by the American people was based upon the certainty of its terms. Immigrants to America were familiar with government tyranny.** What can be called the "second declaration of independence," the first ten amendments protect the people by restricting the power of King George-type individuals should they manage to get an office in our own government.

The *Ordinance* was re-passed and mandated by Congress following the ratification of the new *Constitution*. House approval of the *Ordinance* came on July 21, 1789, and Senate approval came on August 4, 1789. President George Washington signed the law on August 7, 1789.

The same men in Congress who reaffirmed the moral, religious operative of the *Northwest Ordinance* on July 13

1787, also drafted the *Constitution of the United States* document (June 7, 1789, to September 25, 1789). This same Congress also formulated the First Amendment.

> The choice of the Higher Authority, all-powerful Creator over a godless humanistic presupposition as the basis for American legal and political philosophy is both historically accurate and responsible-liberty dependant.

Though misrepresented by liberals in the media and academia, the First Amendment restraint on government is intended to assure moral religions the freedom to flourish and compete with their beliefs in the public arena of ideas. For an in-depth review of this intent, see the excellent history book, *The Myth of Separation,* by David Barton, WallBuilders Press, Aledo, Texas, 1991.

If the distribution or modification of the Constitutional powers is found to be defective, changing it is a right that belongs only to the people. In President Washington's farewell message he addressed the common fraud of a self-righteous judiciary:

> But the *Constitution* which at any time exists, till changed by an explicit and authentic act of the whole People, is sacredly obligatory upon all. If in the opinion of the People, the distribution or modification of the constitutional powers be in any particular wrong, let it be corrected by an amendment [by the people] in the way which the Constitution designates. But let there be no change by usurpation; **for though this, in one instance, may be the instrument of good, it is the customary weapon by which free governments are destroyed. The precedent** [judges assuming this authority in spite of the fact that it is the exclusive right of the people to make such changes] **must** [will] **always greatly overbalance in permanent evil any partial or transient benefit which the use** [judicial license] **can at any time yield.**

Liberals know that Americans would never amend the *Constitution* in support of their agenda. They also realize that representatives elected by the people will not legislate the perversions in American law which they seek. To re-educate Americans and impose an agenda of elitist exploitation, they must get control of the judicial branch of government. So, while claiming to be champions of the people, they work feverishly to prevent appointments of constitutionally sound judges. The defect in their vision blinds them to the real world and the consequences of secularism. As long as judges continue to muzzle God-honoring standards for decency in American law, increases in family breakdown, turmoil among youth, and overloading of our prisons and hospitals must be expected.

In the 1948 case, *Brown v. Board of Education,* the Supreme Court boldly rejected American legal traditions. Their decision reflected the secular commitment to "openmindedness and free inquiry" in "the transformation of society." The judges could and should have based their remedy on the *Declaration of Independence* and the *Constitution.* Instead, psychology and judge-made law became the foundation for future Supreme Court decisions. That event was a giant move in support of government by incalculable and changeable decrees. For additional reading, *The Ideal Element in Law* by Roscoe Pound, is recommended. The book was published in 2002 by Liberty Fund, Indianapolis, Indiana.

On June 25, 1962, in *Engle v. Vitale,* the Court took the first step toward removing God's authority and influence from the public mind. Students were being fed the godless worldview, but prayer and the Bible became taboo.

In dissent, Justice Potter rightly accused the majority of hostility rather than neutrality toward moral religion. On June 17, 1963, in *Madalyn O'Hare* (the well-known missionary for the secular faith) *v. Curlett,* the Court decided that the *Constitution of the United States* should become a force in law against school sanctioned prayer and Bible reading.

University and media liberals and the American Civil Liberties Union continue to wage holy war against any one who does not bow to leftist religio/social/political correctness. Without the leverage of tenured academia and judge-made law they would be harmless. In March of 1987, Federal District Judge Brevard Hand, for example, ruled that some Alabama school textbooks were promoting religion by advocating secular humanism, which is an intolerant religion that opposes moral faith. Liberals unleashed a raging attack of ridicule and contempt against Judge Hand. The Judge had simply refused to twist the *Bill of Rights* and use it against the citizens to whom it is intended to protect. The atheistic worldview is promoted while public prayer and Judeo-Christian symbols are prohibited. This has all the appearances of a nationwide conspiracy consisting of small local leftist conspiracies. Enchanted by a sense of greatness liberals bestow honors on one another and publish the accolades in innocent fashion to the naive public.

On June 24, 1992, the Supreme Court, in a 5 to 4 vote, put the force of law behind the enemies of a God-honoring education. They did so by prohibiting professors and clergy of the moral religions from offering a non-sectarian prayer at public school commencement services throughout the nation. In dissent, Supreme Court Justice Antonin Scalia said, "Our religion-clause jurisprudence [the First Amendment restriction on the use of government power against the people] has become bedeviled by reliance on . . . abstractions that are not derived from, but positively in conflict with, our long-accepted constitutional traditions."

While medical students are being taught that the spiritual nature of man is an important aspect of healing, liberal judges blithely closet the moral law and "In God We Trust" as a legitimate basis for making decisions.

The *Declaration of Independence* and the Preamble to the *Constitution* outline the character of governments which champion responsible liberty.

The Constitution was written to implement and preserve the ongoing extension of those values. The following is a brief of a few of the unique and enduring principles for government established in America. They are numbered to facilitate group discussion. Our Founding Fathers debated and argued over the tiniest word changes when drafting the *Constitution*. The testimony of their deliberations and importance to *Constitution* originalism is voluminous. These very specific Principles arise from the American political philosophy and its Judeo-Christian foundation.

American Principle One

GOD IS THE SOURCE OF ALL
RIGHTS AND THE ENABLER OF LIBERTY

"The Laws of Nature and of Nature's God entitle them . . ."
The Declaration of Independence

This first principle recognizes the Creator as the eternal and all-knowing Ruler of the universe. Our rights come from God rather than government. Belief in the Creator and freedom for the moral religions is central to being American. This principle stands in total contrast to the atheistic-humanist alternative for governing. The greatness of America is a reflection of reality inherent in the theistic perspective for constitutional law—government by written and permanent law rather than government by incalculable and changeable decrees.

The God who gave us life gave us liberty at the same time; the hand of force may destroy, but cannot disjoin them (Thomas Jefferson, "Rights of British America," 1774).

Legislation drafted by the United States Senate and House of Representatives, adding the words "under God" to the American Pledge of Allegiance was signed by President Eisenhower in 1954. In 1964, the Supreme Court rejected a challenge to the law.

In 1954, Congress ordered that "a room with facilities for prayer and meditation . . ." be made available in the United States Capitol. The seventh edition of *The Capitol*, an official publication of the United States Congress, describes the stained glass window of the Congressional Prayer Room:

The history that gives this room its inspirational lift is centered in the stained glass window. George Washington kneeling in prayer . . . is the focus of the composition . . .. Behind Washington a prayer is etched: "Preserve me, O God, for in Thee do I put my trust," the first verse of the sixteenth Psalm. There are upper and lower medallions representing the two sides of the Great Seal of the United States. On these are inscribed the phrases: *annuit coeptis*—"God has favored our undertakings"—and *novus ordo seclorum*—"A new order of the ages is born." Under the upper medallion is the phrase from Lincoln's immortal Gettysburg Address, "This Nation under God." . . . The two lower corners of the window each show the Holy Scriptures, an open book and a candle, signifying the light from God's law, "Thy Word is a lamp unto my feet and a light unto my path" [Psalm 119:105].

The significance of the Judeo-Christian basis for American government, when compared to the doctrine and practice of other beliefs, is that **the Judeo-Christian doctrine advocates that all of the moral religions have the freedom to promote their beliefs in public life.**

When taking their oath of office, the Presidents of the United States, beginning with George Washington, have concluded with the prayerful appeal, "So help me God."

Unless the great God who assisted him [Washington] shall be with me and aid me, I must fail; but if the same omniscient mind and mighty arm that directed and protected him shall guide and support me, I shall not fail—I shall succeed (Abraham Lincoln, Springfield, Illinois, February 11, 1861).

The fundamental principle "under God" justifies the right of all men to be self-governing. This belief also has a beneficial effect upon man's reasoning on all other matters. Men are not mere things which evolved by accident. Belief in the divine origin of man gives essential perspective for establishing a government that is subordinate to the will of the governed—man under God over government. Liberty from tyranny and trust in God's law go hand-in-hand.

"The fear of the LORD [whose Word is truth] is the beginning of wisdom: a good understanding have all they that do his commandments: his praise endureth for ever" (Psalm 111:10).

American Principle Two

THE SPIRITUAL NATURE OF EACH INDIVIDUAL IS HELD AS BEING SUPREMELY IMPORTANT

"All men are created . . . endowed by their Creator . . ."
The *Declaration of Independence*

Man is of divine origin and has a spiritual capacity (to work cooperatively with God) that is superior to secular claims, government, and things material. It is the application of this noble belief in Higher Authority and man's spiritual nature, which holds absurd the secular humanist demand that their atheistic faith be the presupposition for education and the law. Their concept of reality has absolutely no basis for upholding established knowledge, moral absolutes, the right to life or individual soul liberty.

Well aware that Almighty God hath created the mind free; that all attempts to influence it by temporal [worldly] punishments or burdens, or civil [government] incapacitations [tyranny over the mind], tend only to beget habits of hypocrisy and meanness, and are a departure from the plan of the Holy Author of our religion, who, being Lord both of body and mind, yet chose not to propagate it by coercion on either as was in His Almighty power to do so; that the impious presumption of legislators and rulers [government, education systems included] civil as well as ecclesiastical, who being themselves but fallible and uninspired have assumed dominion over [assault] the faith of others, setting up their own opinions and modes of thinking as the only true and infallible [modern day liberal political correctness] . . . (Act for Establishing Religious Freedom, passed in the Assembly of Virginia in 1786, Thomas Jefferson, Governor).

The first elements of morality too may be instilled in their minds; such as, when further developed as their judgements advance in strength [of spirit], may teach them how to work out their own greatest happiness, by showing them that it does not depend on the condition of life in which chance has placed them, but is always the result of a good conscience, good health, occupation, and freedom in all just pursuits (Thomas Jefferson, "Notes on the State of Virginia," 1782).

Mental debasement is the greatest misfortune that can befall a people. The most pernicious of conquests which a state [the people within] can experience is a conquest over that just and elevated sense of its [their] own rights which inspires a due sensibility to insult and injury; over that virtuous and generous pride of character, which prefers any peril or sacrifice to a final submission to oppression, and which regards national ignominy as the greatest of national calamities. The records of history prepared for a MASTER and deserves one (Alexander Hamilton, "The Warning," February 21, 1797).

American Principle Three

IT IS THE ACCEPTANCE OF THE UNIVERSAL
MORAL CODE AND HUMAN EQUALITY
WHICH ASSURE LIBERTY

"We hold these truths to be self-evident, that all
men are created equal, that they are endowed by their
Creator with certain unalienable rights . . ."
The *Declaration of Independence*

This traditional premise in American philosophy emphasizes the God-given equality that men have in a moral and legal sense. This premise is in contrast to the moral relativism and political correctness of the liberal humanist view. The record of human history in the Hebrew-Christian Bible points to the existence of one God and nine commandments for superintending our emotions and moral standards that reflect the fearsome power of truth. Obviously, individuals are not equal to others in size or talent. Justice requires, by God's standards, that every person be recognized as being equal spiritually and therefore entitled to the just protection of unalienable Creator-given rights. This unique American concept rests upon the belief that every life, regardless of race, color, or national origin, is the creation of God.

No free government, or the blessings of liberty, can be preserved to any people, but by a firm adherence to justice, moderation, temperance, frugality and virtue, and by frequent recurrence to fundamental principles (*Virginia Declaration of Rights*, 1776).

The consequence is that the happiness of society is the *first* law of every government. This rule is founded on the law of [man's] nature [established by God]; it must control every political maxim: it must regulate the legislature itself. The people have a right to insist that this rule be observed; and are entitled to demand a moral security [freedom of spirit and conscience] that the legislature will observe it. If they have not the first [freedom of conscience], they are slaves; if they have not the second [moral security], they are, every moment, exposed to slavery (Supreme Court Justice *James Wilson, Lectures*, 1790-1791).

Tis substantially true that virtue or morality is a necessary spring of popular government. The rule indeed extends with more or less force to every species of free Government. Who that is a sincere friend to it, can look with indifference upon attempts to shake the foundation of the fabric? (President George Washington, *Farewell Address*).

Let us enjoy the liberty of the sons of God, but let us take care lest we become accomplices in the diminution of virtue which would menace society if Christianity were to grow weak. What should we do without it? If Rationalism wishes to govern the world without regard to the religious needs of the soul, the experience of the French Revolution is there to teach us the consequences of such a blunder (the appeal of the agnostic Ernest Renan to his agnostic friends, 1866).

The relationship of church (without distinction of sect or party) and state in the United States secures full liberty of religious thought, speech and action, within the limits of public peace and order. . . . [Moral] Religion and [responsible] liberty are inseparable. Religion is voluntary, and cannot, and ought not to be forced. . . . The church [organized religious denominations] as such, has nothing to do with the state except to obey its laws and to strengthen its [the government's] moral foundations; the state has nothing to do with the church except to protect her in her property and liberty; and the state must be equally just to all forms of belief and unbelief which do not endanger the public safety. Church and state are equally necessary, and as inseparable as soul and body, and yet as distinct as soul and body . . . Immigrants accept it as a happy boon, especially those who flee from oppression and persecution abroad. Even those who reject the modern theory [One Nation Under God] enjoy the practice, and would defend it in their own interest against any attempt to overthrow it (excerpts from *Church and State in the United States*, Philip Schaff, 1888).

We know that we have made no discoveries; and we think that no discoveries remain to be made in morality; nor many in the great principles of government, nor in the idea of liberty, which were understood long before we were born, altogether as well as they will be after the grave has heaped its mould upon our presumption, and the silent tomb shall have imposed its law on our pert loquacity (Edmund Burke).

American Principle Four

LIBERTY AND THE PURSUIT OF HAPPINESS,
HUMANITY'S GOAL

"Unalienable rights, that among these are Life,
Liberty and the pursuit of Happiness."
The *Declaration of Independence*

Liberty and life are the gratuitous gifts of heaven. I
shall certainly be excused from adducing any formal
arguments to evince, that life, and whatever is
necessary for the safest of life, are the natural rights of
man. Some things are so difficult; others are so plain,
that they cannot be proved (Supreme Court Justice
James Wilson, Lectures, 1790-1791).

Honor, justice and humanity call upon us to hold,
and to transmit to our posterity, that liberty, which
we received from our ancestors (Resolutions of the
Committee for the Province of Pennsylvania, drafted
by John Dickson, a signer of the *Constitution of the
United States*).

That government is instituted and ought to be
exercised for the benefit of the people; which consists
in the enjoyment of life and liberty, and generally of
pursuing and obtaining happiness and safety (James
Madison in the first session of the U.S. Congress in
proposing the *"Bill of Rights"* amendments to the
Constitution of the United States).

Kings or parliaments could not give the rights
essential to happiness. . . . We claim them from a
higher source—from the King of kings, and Lord of
all the earth. They are not annexed to us by
parchments and seals. They are created in us by the
decrees of Providence . . . It would be an insult on the

Divine Majesty to say that he has given or allowed any man or body of men a right to make me miserable. If no man or body of men has such a right, I have a right to be happy. If there can be no happiness without freedom, I have a *right to be free*. If I cannot enjoy freedom without security of property, I have a *right to be thus secured* (John Dickinson, reply to a Committee in Barbados, 1766).

American Principle Five

EVERY SOUL POSSESSES THE RIGHT TO FREEDOM FROM MONOPOLIES OVER THE DISSEMINATION OF KNOWLEDGE

"Religion, morality, and knowledge, being necessary to good government and the happiness of mankind, schools and the means of education shall forever be encouraged."
Article III, *Northwest Ordinance*

Congress shall make no law respecting an establishment of religion [support moral religion in general, but not one denomination over another], or prohibiting the free exercise thereof; or abridging the freedom of speech, or of the press, or the right of the people peaceably to assemble, and to petition the Government for a redress of grievances (First Amendment to the *Constitution of the United States*).

Be it remembered . . . that liberty must at all hazards be supported . . . and cannot be preserved without knowledge among the people. . . . The people have a right from the frame of their nature, to Knowledge [the range of what has been perceived, discovered, or learned], as their great Creator, who does nothing in vain, has given them understandings, and a desire to know . . .. Let us tenderly and kindly cherish therefore, the means of knowledge. Let us dare to read, think, speak and write. Let every order and decree among the people rouse their attention and animate their resolution. Let them all become attentive to the grounds and principles of government (John Adams, *A Dissertation on the Canon and Feudal Law*, 1765).

From the dissentions among sects [denominations and confessions] themselves arises necessarily a right of choosing and necessity of deliberating to which we will conform, but if we choose for ourselves we must allow others to choose also, and to [do so] reciprocally. This establishes religious liberty (Thomas Jefferson, *Notes on Religion*, 1776).

'To educate a person in mind and not in morals,' Theodore Roosevelt once said, 'is to educate a menace to society.' And that, say an increasing number of educators, politicians and citizens at large, is exactly what is happening in many public schools today (Dr. Michael H. Romanowski, Professor of Education at Ohio Northern University).

Militants intolerant of the moral religions". . . should be sent to the electorate, not to the captive audience of youthful minds. The very definition of practical greatness, which built America, entrusts the educational and political emphasis to the control of the people." The public marketplace of ideas "is a much safer place [for secular missionaries] than providing a [taxpayer-funded] haven [behind public classroom doors] for radicals who are beyond responsibility to the public and emphasize what they want with impunity" (from 11th Judicial District of Iowa Grand Jury Presentment, Problems in Higher Education, December 23, 1968).

The following example is another of many proofs that fixed principles are profoundly American and it demonstrates why it is that classroom instruction must be specific if true learning is to occur. In March of 1825, the board of the University of Virginia passed a resolution for the prioritization of teaching content so essential to integrity, and they listed reliable sources for American principles which should be taught. The resolution that was adopted by the university board was proposed by Thomas Jefferson and James Madison, often called the "Father of the *Constitution*" because of his influence in forming the *Federal Constitution* in 1787. These two men were members of the Board of Visitors. Jefferson was the Rector (or head) of the University of Virginia at the time.

The resolution stated—(1) that all students shall be "inculcated" [instill into their minds] with the basic American principles of government; (2) that "none should be inculcated [indoctrinated] which are incompatible with those on which the *Constitution* of this State, and of the United States were genuinely based, in the common opinion." The way to recognize counterfeit world systems is to know the building blocks of the real world—the universal laws by which consequences, good or bad, are reliably determined.

The faculty had a standard of responsibility and (3) were required to teach positively and affirmatively these unique American principles. Only after they had done so were they to teach the conflicting principles as such, judging them by the soundness of the American principles that served as a basis.

The preamble to the University of Virginia's policy resolution of 1825 states:

> Whereas it is the duty of this board to the government [of the United States] under which it lives, and especially to that [of Virginia] of which this University is the immediate creation, to pay especial attention to the principles of government which shall be inculcated therein, and to provide that none shall

be inculcated which are incompatible with those on which the *Constitution* of this state, and of the United States were genuinely based in the common opinions; and for this purpose it may be necessary to point out specifically where these principles are to be legitimately developed.

The resolution went on to specify six writings (4) that, in the board's opinion, reflected the unanimously supported distinct government principles unique to America with which youth should be indoctrinated. Two of the documents were of an expository nature and known for their clarity in which the ideals of government are amplified and their practical benefits applied to human nature. These were John Locke's *Essay Concerning the True Original Extent and End of Civil Government* (1690) and Algernon Sidney's *Discourses Concerning Government* (1698).

The first four documents referred to were the *Declaration of Independence*, Washington's *Farewell Address*, the *Virginia Resolutions* of 1799 (adopted by the Virginia legislature), and the *Federalist Papers*. These were listed in that resolution as being sound sources of "the general principles and rights of man in nature and society."

Tenure guarantees that empower extremists to impede the transfer of such knowledge is a damning misapplication of government power. "Knowledge of these principles is an indispensable aspect of academic freedom/responsibility which is closely related to individual liberty/responsibility. Otherwise, students are deprived of the substance of their rights to freedom of choice; the right to knowledge is essential for responsible liberty to prevail. Who has academic freedom, the parent/taxpayer or the teacher? Is the parent, who once had academic freedom, now to be deprived because a teacher was hired? Most agree that anyone can teach what he pleases on his own responsibility, but must not yield to his cry of academic freedom and rob taxpayers of their freedom to direct public education in the public's interest, based upon the learning process and established knowledge" (from 11th Judicial District of Iowa Grand Jury Presentment, Problems in Higher Education, December 23, 1968).

American Principle Six

PRIVATE OWNERSHIP OF PROPERTY IS INDISPENSABLE TO LIBERTY

"The right of the people to be secure in their persons, houses, papers, and effects, against unreasonable searches and seizures shall not be violated . . . "
Article IV added as an amendment
to th*e Constitution of the United States*

The great end of government (after the glory of God, is) . . . the good of man, the common benefit of society . . . instituted for the preservation of men's persons, properties and various rights (Reverend Jonathan Mayhew, election sermon, 1754).

And it is necessary that . . . all the powers of Government [should be] exerted, under the authority of the people of the colonies, for the preservation of internal peace, virtue, and good order, as well as for the defense of their lives, liberties and properties (resolution recommending that each colony frame a new government, Continental Congress, May 15, 1776).

The Utopian schemes of leveling, and a community of goods, are as visionary and impracticable, as those which vest all property in the Crown [or government], are arbitrary, despotic, and in our government unconstitutional (House of Representatives, Massachusetts, 1768, to agent in London for the Colonies).

Among the natural rights are these: first a right to life; secondly to liberty; thirdly to property; together with the right to support and defend them in the best manner they can—those are evident branches of, rather than deductions from the duty of self-preservation, commonly called the first law of nature (resolutions of town of Boston, 1772).

American Principle Seven

GROUP RIGHTS ARE LIMITED FOR THE SAKE OF INDIVIDUAL LIBERTY AND NATIONAL SOLIDARITY

"Assume among the Powers of the Earth, the separate and equal station to which the Laws of Nature and of Nature's God entitle them . . ."
The *Declaration of Independence*

All, too, will bear in mind this sacred principle, that though the will of the majority is in all cases to prevail, that will to be right must be reasonable; that the minority possess their equal rights, which equal law must protect, and to violate would be oppression (President Jefferson's First Inaugural Address).

Political liberty is by some defined, the liberty of doing whatever is not prohibited by law. The definition is erroneous. A tyrant may govern by laws . . . Let it be thus defined; political liberty is the right every man in the state has, to do whatever is not prohibited by laws, TO WHICH HE HAS GIVEN HIS CONSENT (this emphasis is part of the original report); ("Essex Result," report of Convention of Towns, Essex County, Massachusetts, rejecting first proposed *Constitution for Massachusetts*, 1778).

For, brethren, ye have been called unto liberty; only use not liberty for an occasion to the flesh [evil impulse], but by love serve one another (from the New Testament book in the Bible, Galatians 5:13).

American Principle Eight

WISDOM DICTATES THAT GOVERNMENT BE FEARED

"In questions of power [government] then, let no more be heard of confidence in man, but bind him down from mischief by the chains of the *Constitution*."
Virginia Resolutions, by Thomas Jefferson

The American people wisely rejected the concoctions of a living *Constitution*. Fear of government is perhaps the third most important of all the principles to which our nation's success is indebted. This principle reflects the ever-present danger that government servants will overreach their authority for the gain of power and personal goals. President George Washington in his *Farewell* warned, "A just estimate of that love of power, and proneness to abuse it, which predominates in the human heart is sufficient to satisfy us of the truth of this position." For this reason government by "incalculable and changeable decrees" was rejected. Before ratifying the *Constitution*, Americans insisted that it be amended by a very specific *Bill of Rights*. Preserving original intent is necessary for the protection of the character of American citizens from paternalistic government schemers. There is a self-serving responsibility to our Benefactor. With the desire to retain our God-given right to be free from tyranny goes the citizenship duty to reject the purveyors of government paternalism and to respect, with moral behavior, the God-given rights of others.

> Show me that age and country where the rights and liberties of the people were placed on the sole chance of their rulers being good men, without the consequent loss of liberty! I say the loss of that dearest privilege has ever followed, with absolute certainty, every such mad attempt (Patrick Henry, Virginia Ratifying Convention, 1788).

There is no danger I apprehend so much as the consolidation of our government by the noiseless, and therefore un-alarming instrumentality of the Supreme Court (Thomas Jefferson, letter to William Johnson, 1823).

Experience hath shewn, that even under the best forms [of government], those entrusted with power have, in time, and by slow operations, perverted it into tyranny . . . (Thomas Jefferson, *Diffusion of Knowledge Bill* in Virginia Legislature, 1779).

American Principle Nine

TAXES ARE LIMITED FOR LIBERTY'S SAKE

"He has erected a multitude of New Offices, and sent
hither swarms of officers to harass our people,
and eat out their substance."
The *Declaration of Independence*

We cannot be secure in our property unless the system for taxation reflects the will and vote of the people. "Let these truths be indelibly impressed on our minds—that we cannot be happy, without being FREE—that we cannot be free, without being secure in our property (John Dickinson, in Pennsylvania Provincial Convention, 1774).

Indeed, we cannot too often inculcate upon you our desires, that all extraordinary grants and expensive measures may, upon all occasions, as much as possible, be avoided. The public money of this country is the toil and labor of the people . . . And we would recommend particularly, the strictest care and the utmost firmness to prevent all unconstitutional draughts upon the public treasury (instructions to town of Braintree, Massachusetts, to their legislative representatives, 1765).

As a very important source of strength and security cherish public credit . . . use it sparingly as possible . . . avoiding likewise the accumulation of debt . . . in time of peace . . . discharge the debts which unavoidable wars may have occasioned, not ungenerously throwing upon posterity the burden which we ourselves ought to bear (President George Washington, *Farewell Address*).

American Principle Ten

GOVERNMENT MUST BE DECENTRALIZED
AND BOUND, WITH ITS POWERS
WIDELY SEPARATED

"True barriers [bulwarks] of our liberty
are our State governments."
President Thomas Jefferson,
First Inaugural Address

Paramount among the lessons of history is that totalitarians are ever present, and that they naturally seek the reigns of government to achieve their personal goals. This was an over-riding concern during constitutional debates. Consequently, our government was organized in a way that imperialistic elitists in key positions would be unable to make the government do their bidding.

The Members of the several State Legislatures, and all executive and judicial officers, both of the United States and of the several States, shall be bound by Oath or Affirmation [provides a basis for identifying officials who are dishonest], to support this *Constitution* (the *United States Constitution*, Article VI (Article II, Section I prescribes the oath for the President).

As to the danger of the Supreme Court's misinterpreting the controlling intent of the *Constitution*:

It will render powerless the checks . . . [and] will become . . . venal and oppressive. . . . If the States look with apathy on this silent descent of their government into the gulf which is to swallow all, we have only to weep over the human character formed uncontrollable by the rod of iron, and the blasphemers of man, as incapable of self-government, become his true historians (Thomas Jefferson, letter to Charles Hammond, 1821).

Liberty and security in government depend not on the limits, which the rulers may please to assign to the exercise of their own powers, but on the boundaries, within which their powers are circumscribed by the *Constitution*. With us, the powers of magistrates, call them by whatever name you please, are the grants of the people . . .. The supreme power is in them [the people]; and in them, even when the *Constitution* is formed, and government is in operation, the supreme power still remains. A portion of their authority they, indeed, delegate; but they delegate that portion in whatever manner, in whatever measure, for whatever time, to whatever persons, and on whatever conditions they choose to fix (U.S. Supreme Court Justice *James Wilson, Lectures*, 1790-1791).

The jurisdiction of the Supreme Court of the United States, or of any other court to be instituted by the Congress, is not in any case to be increased, enlarged, or extended by any Fiction Collusion or mere suggestion (New York Ratifying Convention, 1788, proposed amendments to the *Constitution*).

It is important, likewise, that the habits of thinking in a free Country should inspire caution in those entrusted with its administration, to confine themselves within their respective Constitutional spheres; avoiding in the exercise of the Powers of one department to encroach upon another. The spirit of encroachment tends to consolidate the powers of all the departments in one, and thus to create whatever the form of government, a real despotism. The necessity of reciprocal checks in the exercise of political power; by dividing and distributing it into different depositories, and constituting [establish in the law] each the Guardian of the Public Weal [well-being] against invasions by the others, has been evinced [demonstrated clearly] by experiments ancient and modern; some of them in our country and under our own eyes. To preserve them must be as necessary as to institute them (excerpts from George Washington's *Farewell Address*).

Because it is proper to take alarm at the first experiment on our liberties, we hold this prudent jealousy to be the first duty of citizens, and one of [the] noblest characteristics of the late Revolution. The freemen of America did not wait till usurped power had strengthened itself by exercise, and entangled the question in precedents. They saw all the consequences in the principle [usurped power with unconstitutional precedents], and they avoided the consequences by denying the principle (James Madison, *Memorial and Remonstrance Against Religious Assessments*—addressed to the General Assembly of Virginia, 1785).

The sacred Rights of mankind are not to be rummaged for among old parchments or musty records. They are written, as with a sunbeam, in the whole volume of human nature, by the Hand of the Divinity itself, and can never be erased or voided or obscured by mortal power (the passage is in capital letters in the original, Alexander Hamilton, *The Farmer Refuted*, 1775).

The American system is "a Republic"—"a federation, or combination, of central and State Republics—under which: The different governments will control each other." "Within each Republic there are two safeguarding features: (a) a division of powers, as well as (b) a system of checks and balances between separate departments: Hence a double security arises to the rights of the people" (*The Federalist*, number 51, James Madison).

American Principle Eleven

GOVERNMENT IS TO SERVE AS A TOOL AND A TOOL ONLY

"That to secure these [God-given] rights, Governments [the powers in law to punish violators] are instituted among Men."
The *Declaration of Independence*

Jefferson wrote, "Almighty God has created the mind free." Responsible liberty upon which the freedom to be informed and to estimate the consequences which will follow a particular decision hinge on an absolute source. The Hebrew-Christian Bible is the primary source of this revolutionary idea. Man under God over government, which serves as a tool only, is practical. It is far more advanced in kindness and compassion than having a centrist government with the power to tax the people. All the moral religions, Christian and non-Christian, have the right to share their understanding of truth in public dialog and this, above all else, must be protected. This, along with prayer and a conscientious search of God's Word for the meaning and purpose of life, is the essence of "In God We Trust."

Competition of ideas is opposed by government elitists because competition of ideas is the pathway to public awareness and the adrenalin essential for responsible citizenship.

In this, One Nation Under God, religio/social/political environment citizens have the incentive to make wise choices, and responsible liberty prevails.

> No title of nobility [superior class] shall be granted by the United States [government] (Article 1, Section 8, *Constitution of the United States*).

> For who are a free people? Not those, over whom government is reasonably and equitably exercised, but those, who live under a government so constitutionally checked and controlled, that proper provision is made against its being otherwise exercised (John Dickinson, Political Writings, 1767-1768).

Constitutional deliberations were clothed in the reality of history. The Founding Fathers were not impressed by the arguments of collectivist elites who held out the promise of an earthly utopia. It is God Who gives life and the rights essential for progress, and utopia is the alternative to hell in the hereafter. Government must be structured in a way that man's deception and wickedness toward men be discouraged.

Constitutional deliberations were very serious business. Participants had been labeled traitors and were liable to be hung in a public square from a gallows. Today's secular intellectuals are more cultured. Those who oppose their agenda are enemies because they are infected by decadent beliefs. If they refuse to be re-programmed by government education, they must then, for the purification of society, be exterminated. Some secular elites know exactly where their ideology leads. Others have been duped and live with the illusion of an earthly utopia. This gruesome truth is the dominant secular imprint on world history!

> That the doctrine of non-resistance against arbitrary power and oppression is absurd slavish, and destructive of the good and happiness of mankind

(Virginia Ratifying Convention's proposal for amending the new national *Constitution*, 1778).

The multitude I am speaking of, is the body of the people—no contemptible multitude—for whose sake government is instituted; or rather, who have themselves erected it, solely for their own good—to whom even kings and all in subordination to them, are strictly speaking, servants and not masters (Samuel Adams, essay in *The Boston Gazette*, 1771).

CONCLUSION

The Bible is an exposition of history that focuses upon God's role on behalf of mankind. An accurate picture of history is important because it is the most reliable basis for estimating the different outcomes which can be expected from the options available for action. Having an overview of history, knowing where we best fit into the picture, and full-time confidence in the One Who made it is the essence of life.

The motto, "A NEW ORDER OF THE AGES," on the Great Seal of the United States is most appropriate. For the first time in history an entire nation was/is founded upon a foundation which is both practical and real. The law of our land is the law of nature and nature's God. The unalienable rights which man possesses do not come from legislators or judges; rights which are superior to secular claims, governments and things material come from God. The role of the American *Constitution* is to be an anchorage for written and permanent law based upon the Creator view of reality—the view of reality that concurs with history and man's nature. The role of legislators in this dispensation of God's grace is to do their best to tailor laws which reflect the laws of God and thereby facilitate human progress.

The fifty-six men who signed the *Declaration of Independence* were all victims of manhunts and driven from their homes. Several of the signers lost their wives, children, or their entire family. Nine of them died of wounds or hardships during the war of the Revolution. Five were captured and brutally beaten. The homes of twelve signers were burned, and seventeen lost everything they owned. Not one defected or betrayed his pledge. In contrast today, secularists in our schools and courts of law are working overtime to betray American foundations.

Americans rejected belief in many gods when establishing their government, and "A new order of the ages is born" (the Great Seal of the United States). The concept of Higher Authority is the distinguishing characteristic of the new order. The references to the Commandments given by God to Moses which are on display in our nation's capitol are no accident. Further stated, they are the revolutionary foundation for government by written and permanent law.

That some persons will have strong objections to the words used to express American ideals must be assumed. If the absence of objectors were a requirement, we could not even have a *Constitution*. "One nation under God, indivisible, with liberty and justice for all" clearly reflects the American choice of a theistic rather than an atheistic secular worldview. The belief that providence rests with Higher Authority is the reasoning behind the impartial nature of our *Constitution*. The *Constitution of the United States* concludes with the respectful and affectionate salutation, "In the Year of our Lord."

Some aspirations of mankind are universally distinguishable. One is seen by the fact that the masses continue to flee from nations governed by "incalculable and changeable" decrees to America. This is true even though our nation falls way short of perfection.

When the knowledge of American principles again becomes a focus in our schools (reading, writing, arithmetic, and American principles), the perverse nature of secular humanist dogma will become apparent to American youth.

Renan, though an agnostic, was correct when he wrote to his agnostic friends:

> Let us enjoy the liberty of the sons of God, but let us take care lest we become accomplices in the diminution of virtue which would menace society if Christianity were to grow weak. What should we do without it? If Rationalism wishes to govern the world without regard to the religious needs of the soul, the experience of the French Revolution is there to teach us the consequences of such a blunder.

> On every question of construction [original intent and meaning], carry ourselves back to the time when the *Constitution* was adopted, recollect the spirit manifested in the debates, and instead of trying what meaning may be squeezed out of the text, or invented against it, conform to the probable one in which it was passed (Thomas Jefferson, letter to Justice William Johnson, June 12, 1823). See Thomas Jefferson, *Thomas Jefferson: Writings* —Autobiography, Notes on the State of Virginia, Public and Private Papers, Addresses, Letters, New York: the Library of America, 1984.

The Illusion Of Reality
(Rebellion against God / incalculable and changeable decrees)

Ship Without an Anchor—Education and Laws
Waxing Worse and Worse

In Denial of Truth—
The Godless Relativistic Presupposition

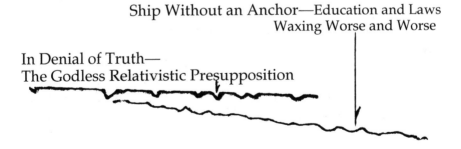

Dumbed down by an education monopoly, America's youth

can be compared with the casualties of military conquest. Many become the victims of ruinous lifestyles, and others actually become troopers for the enemy. This is a tyranny of the worst kind. That continued accommodation of teacher tenure privilege is the enemy of soft science education is self-evident. See The Citizens' Report, page 49, and Public Education Now, pages 75-77.

During deeply troubled times in America what has been the inspiration for renewal? What was the motivation for cohesive responsible action? In addition to the Bible, where have the great leaders of the last two centuries turned? They turned to the *Declaration of Independence*. As knowledge of the *Declaration* came upon the world, it came like a relentless ocean tide. Understanding the substance of the *Declaration of Independence* and the tactics of the atheistic humanism cadre within are the all-sufficient basis for renewal today.

Surveys taken following the September 11, 2001, tragedy suggest that some 90 percent of Americans prayed for our nation and persons affected by terrorists acts, and that 54 percent went to a church, synagogue, or mosque to pray. Though many are confused, Americans understand the importance of traditional American values. They are disgusted with class warfare and denigration of Christians by the political left.

Thankfully, there are now a growing number of non-leftist media organizations, and Americans by the millions are separating themselves from one-sided liberal newspapers, television programs, radio, and churches.

Subscribers to leftist television, radio, and newspaper misrepresentations are nearly half of what they were fifteen years ago, and conservative books are beginning to dominate top-seller lists. This is progress of historic significance!

The major problem which remains is the public school situation where tenure guarantees have empowered

liberals in the soft sciences to dictate what is taught to American youth. Nestled in our universities and the teacher unions, they will never, as long as they have tenure, teach the truth about morality and "One Nation Under God."

Key to our success against the British King and Empire was the activity of citizens who carried the message of the enemy's tactics to their **neighbors, relatives,** and **friends**. As news of the *Declaration of Independence* spread, citizens in communities throughout the colonies wrote and signed their own mini declarations of independence. It is most interesting to study these declarations. It is our responsibility and earnest duty to carry the message to our own New Jerusalem (our neighbors, relatives, and friends), one person at a time. Do not give thought to being embarrassed. When I have taken a clear public stand for American values, the pluses have always outweighed the negatives. As Americans in our communities learn the truth they will reject politicians who promote class hatred and the schools, which are teaching falsehoods about American history, will fade away. It may take up to two four-year election cycles, but that is all that is needed to restore respect for our *Constitution*.

We can win! **Restoring citizen awareness of the foundations summarized in this chapter, and upon which responsible liberty rests, is the key to success.**

Restoring the *Constitution* in its original meaning as the basis for law will in turn restore respect for the citizens' right to control what their youth are taught.

Truth changes the minds of observers like the ripple effect of a pebble landing on water. That is the reason for this chapter on American Principles.